WISDOM CIRCLES

WISDOM CIRCLES

A Guide to Self-Discovery and Community Building in Small Groups

CHARLES GARFIELD,
CINDY SPRING,
AND
SEDONIA CAHILL

NEW YORK

 For information address Hyperion, 114 Fifth Avenue, New York, New York 10011.

Library of Congress Cataloging-in-Publication Data
Garfield, Charles A.
Wisdom circles : a guide to self-discovery and community building in small groups / Charles Garfield, Cindy Spring, and Sedonia Cahill.—1st ed.
p. cm.
Includes bibliographical references.
ISBN 0-7868-6276-9
1. Small groups—Religious aspects. 2. Spiritual life.
3. Wisdom—Religious aspects.
I. Spring, Cindy. II. Cahill, Sedonia. II. Title.
BL628.4.G37 1998
291.6'5—dc21 97-2804
CIP

Designed by Christine Weathersbee

FIRST EDITION
2 4 6 8 10 9 7 5 3 1

Excerpts from *The Heart Aroused* by David Whyte. Reprinted by permission of Bantam/Doubleday/Dell Publishers.

Excerpts from *Out of Solitude* and *With Open Hands* by Henri Nouwen. Reprinted by permission of Ave Maria Press, Notre Dame, IN 46556.

Excerpt from "The Poetic Revelation" from *The Bow and the Lyre* by Octavio Paz, translated by Ruth L.C. Simms, copyright © 1956 by Fondo de Cultura Economica, copyright (c) 1973 by Octavio Paz. By permission of the University of Texas Press.

Excerpts from *The Year I* by Arnold Mindell. Used by permission of the author.

Excerpt from *World as Lover, World as Self* by Joanna Macy. Reprinted with permission of Parallax Press, Berkeley, California.

Quote from Lewis Mumford from *Lapis Magazine* Issue 3. Reprinted by permission of *Lapis Magazine*.

Excerpt from "Ritual Revival and the Circle of Community" by Hollye Hurst. Reprinted by permission of *Creation Spirituality Magazine*.

Excerpt from *Letters to a Young Poet* by Rainer Maria Rilke, translated by M.D. Hewer Norton, translation copyright 1934, 1954 by W.W. Norton & Company, Inc. Renewed © 1962, 1982 by M.D. Herter Norton. Reprinted by permission of W.W. Norton & Company, Inc.

Quote from segment on Buddhism in the video series *The Wisdom of Faith* with Huston Smith and Bill Moyers. Used by permission of Huston Smith.

Excerpt from *The Book of Hours* by Rainer Maria Rilke, translated by Anita Barrows and Joanna Macy, 1996. Reprinted by permission of Putnam Publishing Group.

To Sylvia Garfield, my mother, with love and admiration for spending your wisdom years in the company of kindred spirits. —*C.G.*

To Rita Centkowski, my mother, with love for teaching me the value of meeting with the same group of women monthly for over fifty years. —*C.S.*

To my beautiful grandson, Garrett McDuff, with a prayer that all together we can make the world a safe place for the children. —*S.C.*

CONTENTS

We each contain an enduring spark of that Wisdom
at the heart of all creation. Isolated and unsupported, it is but a small spark. United with others, those sparks grow into a flame of illumination and strength for us all.

That strength which sustains and renews each one of us also
sustains and renews
our communities,
our organizations, our environment, the Earth. Gathering in wisdom circles enables us to move deeply into ourselves, into that core which continues to survive, hope, dream, and carry on.

WISDOM

On Earth Day, twenty-two people gather in a circle in a backyard near wooded hills. As the talking stick is passed around, they speak to the question: How are you consciously participating in the destruction of the environment? There's obvious pain as they tell stories of being stuck in traffic jams, wasting enormous amounts of paper at work, and discarding reparable appliances because no service is available. In the second round, each person tells a tale about what they're doing to help reverse the process of degradation. At the closing ritual, a poem by ecologist John Seed is read that ends with the words: "Fill us with a sense of immense time so that our brief, flickering lives may truly reflect the work of vast ages past and also the millions of years of evolution whose potential lies in our trembling hands."

Sixteen veteran AIDS caregivers spend a January weekend passing the talking stick and telling their best caregiving stories, and their worst nightmares. In the circle they gradually discover how to care for themselves, how to unearth the grief buried beneath the hundreds of deaths they've witnessed, how to consolidate their wisdom, and how to carry on. No one else can guide them. They are their own experts, yet they have had no time to stop, breathe, and reflect.

CIRCLES

Members of a United Church of Christ congregation meet throughout the fall in a series of small dinner gatherings, each followed by a wisdom circle. Over one-third of the congregation participates and addresses the question: In what ways do you express gratitude for the divine abundance in your life? "Having these circles where people can listen and speak from the heart with each other has had a profoundly bonding effect on all of us," says the minister. "For me, this is what spirituality is about."

In an ongoing wisdom circle begun one New Year's Eve, five people address the question: What act of courage could you take right now in order to live your values more fully? One person struggles to say she needs help with alcoholism, another needs the courage to leave a successful job for the work that she passionately wants to be doing, another wants to learn how to live more fully with a life-threatening illness. Each member acknowledges how much they count on this monthly gathering for strength and vision.

INTRODUCTION

In the Company of Kindred Spirits

We are calling a circle and invite you to join with us. We yearn for a safe space within which to be authentic, trusting, caring, and open to change. We are searching for a way of life that embraces wisdom and compassion as its core principles. By "wisdom" we mean deep insight into the interdependence of all phenomena, into the ways we are connected and how the strength of each one of us is vital to the whole. By "compassion" we mean the deep feeling that comes when we recognize our soul's reflection in another person, when that other person's pain or joy becomes our own.

We know that the place to begin is within our own hearts and minds. That is what led us to establish Wisdom Circles. We want to share our efforts in self-discovery, social activism, and spiritual inquiry in the company of kindred spirits. We recognize the advantages inherent in the way the entire ecosystem organizes itself: with an emphasis on interdependence, diversity, and the well-being of future generations. To integrate these values into our daily lives, we need the strength and support of a larger community.

So we invite you to come sit with us in a circle, meeting heart to heart, learning from each other's life experiences and honoring the values that sustain our lives. This is a place for deep truth-telling, for practicing a way of relating to each other that can become the norm for all our relationships. This is also a place for recognizing our own unique talents and abilities. We will pass the talking stick and take turns speaking to our basic inquiry: How can we continue to survive, hope, dream, and carry on during this time of global tumult? Can you listen from the heart without judgment, without resistance, to the urgencies of a soul longing to be heard? Can you speak from the heart, expressing your truth as best you know it? And will you choose your words carefully, with sensitivity to their impact? Can you express gratitude to those who bear witness to your words? Will you sit in silence and wait for deeper thoughts and feelings to rise? Can you give voice to this new form of community pressing to be born?

Our Heritage of Circles

The circle is an ancient and universal symbol for unity and wholeness. For many millennia human beings have met in tribal or village circles to tell stories, provide mutual support, and arrive at an understanding of the common good. The political foundations of North America were shaped primarily by two strong circle traditions: the British and the Native American. One of Britain's most enduring stories, originating in Celtic mythology, is that of King Arthur and his Round Table. The knights took an oath to serve not only the other table members but the kingdom as a whole. Their covenant promised a humane safety net for even the most vulnerable members of society.

When we read about the history of the U.S. Constitution, we learn that it was based fundamentally on the model of the Iroquois Confederacy, a system of separate tribal councils that met as a Grand Council every five years *with the responsibility for the welfare of the whole*. Members of the tribal councils were chosen by the Council of Matrons, the oldest women of the tribe, who met in a circle.

Since the times when people sat around the tribal fire, we have developed many variations of the circle: support groups, dialogue groups, group psychotherapy, Bible study groups, twelve-step groups, consciousness-raising circles, men's and women's groups, to name a few. According to a recent study funded by the Gallup Foundation, 40 percent of all adult Americans actively belong to small, voluntary groups whose purpose is to explore what has meaning in their lives and address urgent social concerns. Research sociologist Paul Ray concludes that there are as many as 44 million adults in the United States who share values consistent with wisdom circles and are actively pursuing personal and social transformation. "However, these people have been like an audience all facing the same direction, reading the same stuff," Ray says, "sharing the same views, but not facing one another." It is time for us to come together in small groups that share the same goal: the creation of a compassionate community that values the wisdom and the welfare of all its members. A compassionate community of people who are willing to sustain our gaze upon suffering, upon the wounds that we inflict upon one another and upon the earth, and who are willing to become accountable for their actions.

How Did Wisdom Circles Begin?

In the course of writing this book, we three authors gathered in a wisdom circle to discuss our personal history with small groups. Each one of us came to the circle from a different background.

Cindy Spring: My initial motivation for starting Wisdom Circles came during a vision quest in the Nevada desert led by Sedonia. For years I had been looking for a way to make my work more meaningful. I wanted to regain my faith in humankind and the determination to make a difference—values that I had held as a social activist in the 1960s. During that week in the desert, I came to understand the power that circles have to create community and to plumb the depths of our experience. I discovered new levels of honesty in myself I hadn't known. The circles formed during the vision quest both supported and challenged me more than the consciousness-raising groups I was used to. I came away with a new mission: to encourage people to meet in circles and then find a way to network those circles. I asked my husband, Charlie, and Sedonia to join me, and in 1994 we founded an organization called Wisdom Circles to promote a wider understanding of the power of circles and the circle process.

Since then, I've been a circle maker in a wide variety of settings—at conferences, in organizations, and in groups that I've seeded with others. An ecology group I belong to—the Women's Forest Sanctuary—has an ongoing wisdom circle. I've helped to integrate the wisdom circle format into the viewers' guide for a PBS series called *Reaching Out* that focuses on the role of community service in relation to racism and to the assault on the environment. I've answered hundreds of letters from people around the country asking for more information.

The earliest influence I had to go in this direction stems from my mother. She has been meeting monthly with the same group of seven women since 1941. I grew up with that "circle" meeting being held often in my house, and I saw at close range how important a group like that can be in your life.

CHARLIE GARFIELD: I grew up in Brooklyn in the late 1940s, when Jews were so profoundly wounded by the Nazi Holocaust. Everything in our community was colored by our soul connection to the survivors who escaped and to the many millions who perished. The Holocaust forged a capacity for deep feeling in me. Later, as a child of the post-Sputnik era, I was channeled into math and computer science and ended up working on Apollo Eleven, which made our first moon landing. Ironically, that technological achievement taught me a lot about our human capacity for inspired collaboration. So I followed an urge to find work that was more people-oriented, and that led to a doctorate in psychology.

In 1974 I founded Shanti Project, which is a volunteer-based organization that provides support for people with life-threatening illnesses. Shanti later became one of the first community-based AIDS agencies in the nation. The circles we held for volunteers and for people with cancer and AIDS were much like wisdom circles, since we emphasized speaking and listening from the heart. We never could have done such challenging work without mutual support.

During the 1980s, I wrote about high-achievers and helped redefine our notion of a "peak performer," a shift from an independent operator to someone who is a fully participating partner in a group or organization. AIDS work is really about community, and caregivers are doing some of the most magnificent work anywhere. When Cindy asked me to join her in Wisdom Circles, it was a natural fit for me. I realized that here was a way to meet with people that went beyond support groups, something I could take into a variety of settings, wherever there was a need for people to share their feelings, tell their truths, and listen from the heart.

My greatest satisfaction has come from introducing wisdom circles into the AIDS caregiving community throughout the country. Many caregivers and people with HIV/AIDS have been hit so hard by the disease that their hearts were already opened and the wisdom circle format suited their needs well. Wisdom circles have also been received well by health professionals, who are facing the turmoil of health-care reform. Health care in the United States is in flux, and people often don't have the chance to communicate their thoughts and feelings honestly. Many health-care professionals are shell-shocked by the changes and are struggling to redefine their roles and hold onto their sense of a caregiving mission.

A wisdom circle gives people a unique opportunity

for self-disclosure, and I value that more than any single aspect of the process they entail. I'm most aware of their contribution when I can ask: "What is the deeper truth for us in this context?" I've been able to pose that question when I consult with corporations, asking their members: "If we went deeper than what we're saying, what's the *real* truth? What's the reality you wish you could give voice to but you never believed you could risk saying?" It's heartening to see how they respond. People have an intuitive sense of how vital truth-telling is. It's wonderfully empowering to see a group of people who are locked up in fear and by what they believe are the limits of their corporate culture, finally begin to tell the truth. When they trust that I'm able to hold a safe place with them, they begin to honestly examine their work and its relation to their lives.

SEDONIA CAHILL: When I was attending Sonoma State University in 1981, to get my master's degree in psychology, I was going through a very difficult and confused time personally. I had just ended a painful relationship and was also in a midlife crisis. In one of my classes, we met in circle, used the talking staff, and were expected to speak in a very personal way. At that time I was so blocked I could hardly speak out loud. In those circles, you shared what you had to say in a singing voice with your own melody. Singing felt way past what I was capable of. I had a hard time participating, but I managed to.

I had been sitting in circles since the 1960s, particularly in consciousness-raising groups with women. We shared a lot, but the circles at Sonoma State were different. Their sacred context challenged me to go deeper than I'd ever been able to. Those circles changed my life. I found that I could express what was most deeply inside me. The circle was the key to unlocking myself.

Shortly after that, I started a women's circle that's still meeting. I believe that one of the spiritual challenges we each face is to create a circle in our hearts that is very large and inclusive. It means questioning ourselves about who and what we feel kinship with, who and what is in our life circle, and about who we feel alienated from and who we exclude.

The circle is my spiritual path. I use circles in my vision quest work—it's the heart of it. I've traveled all over the United States and Canada, to the Ukraine and Australia, helping people start circles. I've been in special one-time circles that honored rites of passage and life events such as births, marriages, menopause, and divorce. And also circles that met only one or two times to explore aging, gender issues, and relationships. We've held large drumming circles to help other circles start. My women's circle is responsible for seeding more than fifty circles in Northern California. I've led ongoing circles in women's prisons and women's recovery houses, and I belong to a listening council that is made up of delegates drawn from eight different local circles. We offer a service to the community—a place where people can bring their issues and conflicts and work toward solutions.

How Wisdom Circles Work

Those of us drawn to wisdom circles are linked by a vision of a more humane and sustainable future for us all. We're beginning to observe our evolutionary journey, assess whether it is in harmony with life on earth, make conscious choices, and take responsibility for contributing to a world that works for everyone. Our intention, then, as circle participants, is to engage each other at increasingly deeper levels of wisdom and compassion. To do so, it is paramount that we learn how to share our stories and experiences. Stories are the language of community.

The circle is open and closed with a simple ritual of the group's choosing. A topic is chosen by the members and is sometimes posed in the form of a question, and we take turns responding in a "round." The speaker holds a talking stick or other symbolic object and speaks without interruption; there is no advice given, no cross-talk. Listening is the primary activity. We value silence as much as words, and empower each person to be a co-facilitator.

Wisdom circles are places to practice heart-to-heart communication skills, to heal wounds, to find the courage to act upon that "still small voice within." Places to share a vision, define a mission. Places where we can create a community, where we can learn to be more fully ourselves, while simultaneously becoming an integral part of the group. Our basic orienting question—"What can we learn from our own and each other's experiences?"—has wide application in support groups, study groups, and organizations of all kinds. Besides the settings we've already mentioned, the wisdom circle format is being used by members of the Institute of Noetic

Sciences, in Unitarian-Universalist and United Church of Christ groups, by hospice nurses, diversity trainers, social activists, corporate work teams, a medical school staff, and a single fathers' group, to name a few.

This simple form has brought understanding and a more profound feeling of community to an amazingly diverse number of groups: to a multiracial group grappling with issues of racism; to executives of a large U.S. corporation demoralized by rapid change; to men in prison; and to hospice nurses working at a major university hospital. What this suggests is that the format has an integrity of its own that speaks to something basic in all human beings. It has the potential to facilitate communications among people who see themselves as very different.

The wisdom circle also serves many of us who have been following a solitary spiritual path and who now feel the need to continue our journey in the company of kindred spirits. These relationships help us to sustain an honest self-inquiry and to counteract those tendencies toward despair, cynicism, and self-doubt that we all experience at times. By listening and speaking from the heart, we enter a realm where real communion can take place. By developing these capacities through practice, we can begin to respect our differences based on race, gender, ethnicity, sexual orientation, class, religion, and political ideology. We can begin to heal the wounds that ail our souls and fragment our society.

The Ten Constants

No two wisdom circles are alike, yet there are elements that all wisdom circles share. The wisdom circle is shaped by a set of guidelines called the Ten Constants. This format has been inspired by councils of indigenous peoples, informed by support and dialogue groups, and drawn from our own experience. We've also investigated group relations theory, mediation techniques, and circle-forming traditions such as Quaker meetings.

We want to help you create and sustain your own circle, using the Ten Constants. A set of guidelines, they also reflect the intentions of a wisdom circle—the shared values and deep purposes common to all wisdom circles, no matter what their individual aims are. For example, *expressing gratitude* and *acknowledging our interdependence* are basic to every wisdom circle. Because it is useful to learn "the basics" in any endeavor, we've devoted a chapter to each of the constants. We ask you to read these chapters slowly. The better you grasp the constants, the more confidence you will feel in leading and participating in your own group. Later, you may choose to modify these guidelines, depending on the needs of your circle. We encourage you to improvise, go with the Muse. Each person is a teacher in the circle, but it will become clear that the real teacher is the circle itself.

Please keep in mind that there is no rigid or "correct" order to the constants:

Honor the circle as sacred time and space by using simple rituals to mark the opening and closing.

Create a collective center by mutually agreeing upon a topic or intention.

Ask to be informed by our highest human values such as compassion and truth, by the wisdom of the ancestors, and by the needs of those yet to be born.

Express gratitude and heartfelt appreciation for the blessings and teachings of life.

Create a safe container for full participation and deep truth-telling.

Listen from the heart, and serve as a compassionate witness for the other people in the circle.

Speak from the heart and from direct experience.

Make room for silence to enter.

Empower each member to be a co-facilitator of the process.

Commit to an ongoing relationship with the people in your group, and carry the intentions of the circle into daily life.

You may find that some of these guidelines are easy to relate to, while others are more challenging. Our advice is to incorporate the constants into your circle at a pace that is comfortable. Listening from the heart and speaking from the heart require considerable empathy and trust. What you look for in the beginning is one or more people who can model "from the heart" for the others. Factors such as one's personal experience with groups, psychological defenses, current life issues, gender, age, race, ethnicity, and economic status can all affect how comfortable a person feels. Part of the group's spiritual work is to help each member feel safe and valued enough to participate.

How to Use This Book

Part 1, Chapters 1–10, outlines the Ten Constants, which provide practical guidelines and embody the intentions of the wisdom circle. Part 2, Chapters 11–16, gives you more insight into the process: how to start, how to deepen the experience, and how to address obstacles that can impede the group's flow. We will go into more detail on how to cultivate a bond among members and consider the types of questions most often posed in wisdom circles. We will describe the many roles that people play in groups—the leader, the resident guru, the quiet one, the victim, the visionary. Chapter 17 offers our visions for wisdom circles and the role of circles in the larger community. In every chapter you will find stories and insights gleaned from other circles. Given our commitment to confidentiality, the names and some details in the stories have been changed.

In addition, we obtained permission from people to use stories that contained particularly intimate details.

Please note that using the wisdom circle format is free of charge and that there is no need to affiliate with any organization or adhere to any doctrine. We hope this book serves you well in starting a wisdom circle of your own or enhancing the circles you already belong to. Most important, we hope this book helps you to extend the values of compassionate community into the Circle of Life.

PART ONE

THE TEN CONSTANTS

ONE

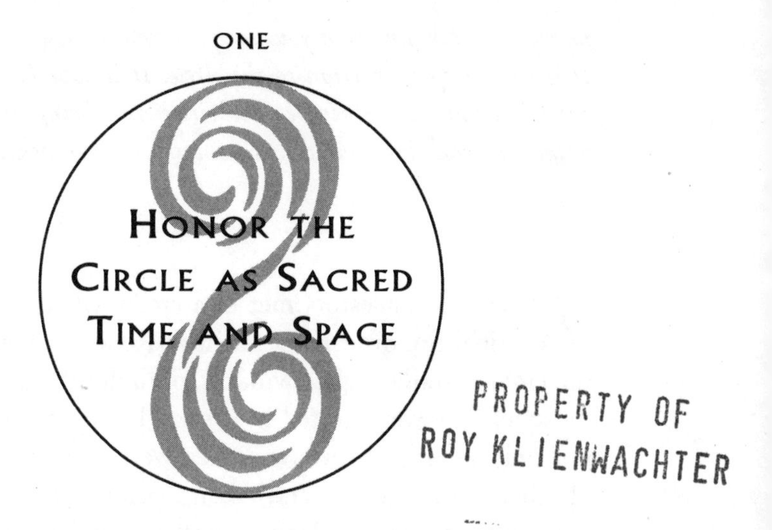

Honor the Circle as Sacred Time and Space

I live my life in widening circles
That reach out across the world.

—*Rainer Maria Rilke,* The Book of Hours

Welcome to the circle. Let's proceed to clear a place for Spirit to enter and take a moment to feel our soul connections. Close your eyes and notice your breathing. Allow your breath to carry you deeper and deeper into yourself, far, far back into time. Into a time when your ancestors met in circles. Perhaps you can hear the drums, feel the warmth of the tribal fire on your face, feel the bonds of kinship and belonging. Each and every one of us had ancestors who sat around a fire together, drumming, singing, dancing, telling stories, praying to the spirit of the sacred place on Earth that they knew as home. In those circles people spoke from the heart, they found solutions to their problems, they laughed and they played, celebrated and grieved together. The memory of this time is in your body, in your bones, in your belly. It is your deep connection to the circle. It is your heritage. The time has come to remember the circle and bring this way of gathering back into our consciousness, into our lives, and into community.

~

When our ancestors met in a circle, whether around a tribal fire or at King Arthur's Round Table, beneath the circular stained-glass window, or under the dome of the mosque, they were united by a sacred purpose. They were not only serving themselves, they were serving the whole of their community and their vision of the divine. Consciousness of the sacred means consciousness of the One—no separations. In a wisdom circle we set up an environment to invite in that consciousness and trust that it may grace us with its presence.

Constant One asks us to honor the circle as sacred time and space. To "honor the circle" means to acknowledge that the circle itself has power as well as people in it. This observance is what distinguishes a wisdom circle from other ways of meeting in circle. Through the use of an opening ritual, we begin with an acknowledgment of the form: We recognize the power of the circle to shape our experience, and we embrace the values it represents. Unity. Wholeness. Reverence for Life and for every manifestation of Life.

Temenos

The power of the circle deepens when "honoring the circle" includes the desire to make it "a sacred time and place." Greek philosophers called it a *temenos*—a sanctuary in which we feel our connection to Spirit, and to the eternal. Ordinary surroundings and routine fade into the background, and we experience a heightened awareness of present time. The Greeks, and people of many other cultures, felt that certain places were a better *temenos* than others. Over the centuries, a grove of trees, a grotto, a hilltop were chosen as sites for spiritual gatherings. Later, temples and cathedrals were built on those sites by other cultures. These places still invite an encounter with the sacred.

Like ancient peoples, we thirst for this experience of the sacred, whereby we remember that true reality lies in our unity with all life. We need the relief of knowing that we can escape, if only briefly, the "chaos" of ordinary life and our sense of being separate and isolated from each other. We, too, need a *temenos* where we connect with the Source of Life. That sense of connection extends outward to include all expressions of life—the trees; the birds; the animals; the running and still waters; the mountains and the deserts; and, lest we forget, all our fellow humans as well.

In *temenos*, you have a feeling of centeredness, of being focused on the present. There is no need to rush. So much of our personal time is spent trying to cope with suffering rooted in the past or attempting to fashion an improved future. We lose sight of the here and now. But as Vietnamese Buddhist monk Thich Nhat Hanh points out, we must take time to fully experience life and see deeply into the present moment, where life has always to be met and lived.

Ritual

Rituals consist of evocative words and symbolic actions; they are meant to invoke *temenos* in any location, even one as ordinary as your living room. In indigenous cultures, rituals honor divine forces thought to bring the daylight; they cause crops to grow and healing to occur. Even though you may not use the word "ritual," you have many of them in your life. Holidays, birthdays, events surrounding births and deaths—these are all occasions for rituals that bind us to each other. Baptisms, graduations, baby showers, and marriages can also be rituals that create what philosopher Huston Smith calls "a sense of ultimate belonging."

Rituals often have meanings that can be difficult to put into words. How would you describe the significance of blowing out candles on a cake? Or putting lights on an evergreen tree? Consider the power of Fourth of July fireworks or the presence of a coffin at a funeral service. Symbolic actions may be more potent than words in stirring our emotions and opening us to that sense of unity. When done mindfully, they can gain even more power through repetition over years or centuries.

When we open and close a wisdom circle with a ritual, we rely on a universal and long-standing practice. Ritual satisfies a deep human need—that is, to regain our sense of reverence and awe, of being connected to something larger than ourselves. According to scholar Joseph Campbell, the idea of a circle having 360 degrees, which we inherited from the Sumerians, has a sacred significance. Campbell says, "The official Sumerian year was three hundred and sixty days with five holy days that don't count, which are outside of time and in which they had ceremonies relating their society to the heavens." Many spiritual traditions have individual practices for stepping out of time—meditation, prayer, altered-state experiences such as fasting, or solo retreats to the desert or mountains. Rituals for a group experience of *temenos* range from the simple lighting of candles, as in the Kwanzaa or Hanukkah celebrations, to the many days of chanting in ashrams in India and the Sun Dance among the Plains Indians of North America. For your wisdom circle, we suggest you choose a simple opening ritual that begins the process of connecting members of the group. As with all rituals having sacred intent, it lays the groundwork for a shift in consciousness from "I" to "We," from the individual to the group.

Discovering how to sit in a circle with people we do not know well, or with those who we might perceive as being different from us, is a profoundly spiritual task. It requires an environment that lends itself to listening deeply and speaking authentically. To begin to lay the bedrock of trust in our wisdom circle, we need to commit to being present for each other. We need to be *mindful*, to remember what we experienced in the past, to discover what is both limiting and inspiring our hopes and dreams today, and to dig for the resiliency and vision to carry on tomorrow. Stepping out of "ordinary time" through ritual gives us more access to that continuum of time in our lives, and it opens the door to a sense of deep communion with self and others.

Most of the time I don't live with an awareness of the sacred, but I do have glimpses of it. It happens in those moments of deep knowing that I am part of a larger whole involving all living beings. It's simple and it's profound. It fills me with joy and peace. Certain situa-

tions offer those glimpses more than others. A walk through a redwood forest, a tender moment with my husband, looking out my window and seeing the deer family in the yard, and a moment of communion with the others in my wisdom circle—these are windows to the sacred for me.

Suggestions for Opening Rituals

People who arrive to participate in a wisdom circle have come from all sorts of "noisy" experiences. They may have just left a highly stressful work situation or a traffic jam, or they've "got things on their mind." A simple ritual helps to shake loose such distractions and allows us to focus on the present. The most common ritual is lighting candles, an effective way of acknowledging that inner spark of wisdom we are seeking to discover and share. Listening to someone recite one of the invocations in this book, or any other appropriate text, sharing some quiet music, drumming, holding hands, sharing the smell of sage or some other fragrance, spending a few minutes in which each person simply focuses on their breathing—any one of these shared experiences can begin the process of aligning the members of the group, bringing them together on a physical and emotional level.

To effectively invoke *temenos*, the opening ritual must also have *meaning* for everyone present. It must help make the connection between self and other apparent. (In Chapter 12, we offer a list of suggestions that help identify the rituals that will be most useful for your group.)

Some rituals don't need explanations; their significance is obvious. Others, such as burning dried sage, might strike some people as strange, even after they are told that certain native cultures use this as a purification ritual. For other people, the sage may remind them of a stay in the desert or harken back to an experience in which incense was used in a church or temple. Even if the experience is entirely new, it may feel appropriate, so trust your intuition.

Rose went to Oregon to take part in a memorial service for her long-time friend, Angelo, who died suddenly in an accident. His close friends and family called for a day-long memorial in an open field near where he had lived. Having discovered that "nothing special" was planned for the gathering, Rose spoke to some of Angelo's relatives at breakfast in the morning. Would they consider having a wisdom circle? Since they weren't familiar with the process, she did a mock circle around the table, using a fork for the talking stick. They liked the idea and said she could lead the service.

Rose opened the circle of more than a hundred people by simply lighting a candle and asking each person to think about their relationship with Angelo. As the talking object, they passed a string of beads that had been precious to Angelo, and each person shared a memory of their beloved friend. In the circle were an uncle who had been present at his birth, two of his brothers, and the man who found Angelo dead after he'd fallen doing some tree work. The circle was a time both to grieve and to celebrate a life. Rose said: "When we closed the circle, we felt that we all knew who this man had been and how loved he was."

A Word of Caution about Rituals

Be aware that some symbols are loaded or negatively charged for certain individuals. For instance, passing a Christian Bible around the circle might be fine for some people but might make others uncomfortable if not everyone in the group is Christian. There are so many possibilities for opening and closing rituals that in the spirit of the circle, it makes sense to find or create those that feel good to everyone. We encourage you to try a variety of opening and closing rituals. During the first year or so, innovate, modify, and vary the rituals you use. The goal is to develop a repertoire that will invoke *temenos* as an environment for the group. As your wisdom circle continues to meet over time, favorite rituals will begin to stand out as inspiring and meaningful to everyone.

Working with rituals is a gentle yet demanding art. As your skill develops, so too does the power of the rituals. If you get too dogmatic about the form, you risk falling into superstition. A wonderful teaching parable, told in *Soul Food: Stories to Nourish the Spirit and the Heart*, edited by Christina Feldman and Jack Kornfield, shows the pitfall of getting stuck in the trappings of ritual:

> *When the guru sat down to worship each evening, the ashram cat would get in the way and distract worshipers. So he ordered the cat be tied during evening worship. After the guru died the cat continued to be tied during evening worship. And when the cat expired, another cat was brought to the ashram so that it could be duly tied during evening worship. Centuries later, learned treatises were written by the guru's scholarly dis-*

ciples on the liturgical significance of tying up a cat while worship is performed.

Remember, the map is not the territory. If a candle goes out or someone spills coffee on the cloth covering the center table, that's okay. It will not incur the wrath of the Furies. And be sure not to equate *sacred* with *solemn*. Laughter and playfulness are also important ways of bonding a group if they occur in the spirit of deep respect of one for another and for life. We each connect with the sacred on a very personal basis. A momentary encounter with the sacred in a wisdom circle may occur for one person and not another. Once in a while the feeling is unanimous.

Expanding Sacred Space and Time into Daily Life

We can set the environment for entering sacred space simply by consciously deciding to do so. This may seem a radical idea at first, but it is anchored in the reality that every square inch of the earth is sacred. Like peoples all over the world, we may feel that certain spots evoke a feeling of *temenos* more than others. But the truth is that all of existence is sacred, and its sacredness is but there for us to recognize it. Given how easy it is for our awareness to stay lodged in the material world, ritual helps us to remember that we are spiritual beings as well.

It is our hope that connecting with the sacred becomes a practice not only in your circle but in your daily life. We encourage you to find those places that evoke *temenos*, or hold spiritual power, for you. Identify those places on earth that bring you closer to that sense of "ultimate belonging."

Create such a place within your home, and honor it with a special table or artifact. Let it be a place for making the sacred palpable by meditating or praying there, on a regular basis.

Now it is time to reclaim together our power to enter sacred time and space by sitting together in circle.

SUMMARY OF CONSTANT ONE:

Honor the circle as sacred time and space by doing simple rituals to mark the circle's opening and closing. Light candles, or take a few moments to breathe deeply and meditate. Burn some incense or sage. Listen to a selection of evocative music or a guided meditation. You can be as creative as you want with these rituals.

There cannot be wisdom without an encounter with the holy, with that which creates awe, and shakes the ordinary way of life and thought. Without the experience of awe in the face of the mystery of life, there is no wisdom.

—*Paul Tillich,* The Eternal Now

TWO

Create a Collective Center

One can not pursue happiness; if he does he obscures it. If he will proceed with the human task of life, the relocation of the center of gravity of the personality to something greater outside itself, happiness will be the outcome.

—*Robert A. Johnson,*
He: Understanding Masculine Psychology

We gather around the flame of wisdom's light and warmth to discover what gifts we've brought with us and what we've learned from our time on Earth. This circle marks the center of the world, our world in this moment. Let this center focus our hearts and minds and connect us to each other. It gives us the power to shift our consciousness from our individual existence to the larger web of life. It is here we begin to know ourselves as members of a group and begin to feel the group within ourselves.

After the opening ritual, circle members each told a story about how they got their names. One man said he'd been given the name Gilmore James Hutchison. He had been named after a grandfather. For most of his life, he was called Jim—until recently. Two years ago he decided to reclaim the name Gilmore. His grandfather, whom he loved dearly, had married a gentle woman named Naomi. Right after Jim started using the name Gilmore, he met and married a woman named Naomi. She was also present in the circle and explained that just before she and Jim had met, she had changed her name from Debbie. Married as Gilmore and Naomi Hutchison, they now bore the names of the two beloved grandparents.

Everyone in the room felt the magic of this story and opened their hearts to the attractive couple. During the next round, Gilmore revealed that he had AIDS. Naomi knew this, of course, but any mention of it was painful. She burst into tears. As Gilmore talked about what he was trying to do to heal himself, and about how much he loved Naomi, their pain became the group's pain. During those moments, the fifteen people who had entered the room as strangers, became united in a single focus, a single story. The group held this couple in its heart.

~

The second constant of wisdom circles has to do with enlarging our sense of self. In the story above, individuals found themselves reacting to the story of Gilmore and Naomi as if it were their own. In those few moments, the boundaries between self and other softened. We went beyond sympathy to deep empathy—identifying with Gilmore and Naomi as if we *were* them.

What does it take for us to shift our awareness for a moment from our individual dramas and forget ourselves? It usually takes something that moves us deeply and touches our hearts. We open up and expand our capacity to feel for and with others.

Most of the time we perceive ourselves to be solitary "I's," bounded by our bodies and limited by our senses. Occasionally we may lose ourselves in the rapture of love-making, or during a music concert, sporting event, or stroll in an ancient forest, or by immersing ourselves in a creative project. People of many cultures willingly blur their ego boundaries by entering into "altered states" through meditation, prayer, intense dancing or drumming, or through the use of psychoactive drugs.

In modern psychology, what we sense as our identity and the agent of our actions is referred to as the "self." That "self," we feel, is the center of our existence. It is "the skin-encapsulated ego," as philosopher Alan Watts put it. But we've each had moments when that center felt larger than our finite selves—when we've surrendered ourselves to love, to nature, to the world of a child, to the experience of the sacred. A wisdom circle can provide an opportunity for this kind of expansion of center as well.

Getting Out of the Hole We're In

Cartoons often contain simple truths, like the one that shows a group of people trapped in a large hole. They each try to jump out, but the hole is too deep. They each try flapping their arms to fly out, but to no avail. They sit down, hoping to be rescued, but no one comes. Finally, they form a human ladder, and each person climbs up the side to the top. Now, what has happened here? A shift of consciousness from "I" to "We" has in fact been illustrated, a shift that can happen pretty quickly in an emergency. We hear of those stories of "we-ness" after a tragedy or disaster—stories of people not thinking, but just jumping in to save another, acting from some instinct seemingly more powerful than self-preservation, acting from the sense that we are all one. But what about those "ordinary times," when there are no immediate threats to contend with? Most of us remain identified with a circumscribed sense of self because we've been conditioned by our culture to consider ourselves distinct and separate entities.

As senior vice-president of operations for a multinational company, I had an impossible task. We went through a tremendous restructuring within a two-year period and had practically an entire new executive team. Confusion and demoralization were rampant and so bad that they threatened to kill the company. I decided to introduce wisdom circles as a way of getting people to tell the truth about what they were feeling. We've prided ourselves for over a century on having strong individual performers and it was clear to me that we were each sinking individually, day by day.

We tried a few wisdom circles in several divisions. They worked so well even the senior executives agreed to do one. That sold them on the concept and we're taking it out in stages to the thousands of our employees.

During the last four hundred years of human history, tremendous emphasis has been laid on the development of the individual. Wise teachers have encouraged us to know ourselves, trust our inner authority, try the road not taken, and fulfill our potential. Western psychology has given us a body of literature on why we need to "individuate," that is, search for the essence of our own uniqueness. Unfortunately, any asset pushed too far becomes a liability. We are seeing the results of this radical emphasis on individualism in our estrangement from the natural world, in our indifference to mass suffering, in the greed of the few at the expense of the many.

The Emergence of the Eco-Self

We have put forth the somewhat radical notion that our sense of self is actually more fluid than we think. Rather than being limited to the concerns of the ego, we can have what psychologist Abraham Maslow called "a sense of self that extends beyond one's egoic, biographic, or personal sense of self" or experience what psychologist-philosopher William James described as "giving your little private convulsive self a rest, and finding that a greater Self is there." Within a wisdom circle we have the opportunity to experience this greater self, this expanded center, a center that includes each of us within the group as a whole. Our intention as stated in Constant Two is to "create a collective center," or, in other words, create a context in which we experience a larger sense of self.

Psychologist James Hillman says that where you make the cut between self and other is always arbitrary. You could define your "self" as the "skin-encapsulated ego," an awareness of yourself held within the vessel of your body. Or you could define your self relative to the context of your relationships, your environment, and your culture. According to Hillman, "We can make [the cut] at the skin or we can take it out as far as you like—to the deep oceans and distant stars." Deep-ecologist Joanna Macy calls the consciousness that extends the self beyond the skin the *ecological self* or *eco-self.*

Much is being written these days on the development of an "eco-consciousness" that would encourage people to extend their sense of self to include the natural world and to consciously participate in the "Web of Life." When ecologist John Seed was asked how he deals with despair in his attempts to save the rainforests of the world he replied: "I try to remember that it's not me, John Seed, trying to protect the rainforest. Rather, I am part of the rainforest protecting itself. I am that part of the rainforest recently emerged into human thinking."

What a wonderful sensibility! None of us (the authors) was reared in a tribal or animistic culture, but we are each trying to cultivate a sense of being embedded in nature, of being one with the natural world. It is indeed hard to look at a tree and see ourselves as an extension of it. The wisdom of those who are urging us to bond with (or reconnect to) the forests, with the oceans, with all life on the planet is clear: We are destroying other forms of life simply because we look at them as something "other," something we feel separate from, and by damaging the Web of Life we are killing ourselves. Eco-consciousness means taking the interests of more and more life forms as *self*-interest and hopefully averting the ecological catastrophe that seems inevitable if we continue to poison, defoliate, and kill off our fellow species.

It is an immensely challenging process to shift one's consciousness away from some of the core values of our time—consumerism, the myth of progress, and the pursuit of narrowly defined personal goals. Our task is to learn such "eco" values as voluntary simplicity, collaboration, and respect for diversity, and to deeply root them in our consciousness so that we can speak to them and act on them.

The good news is that we are, in fact, responding by gathering in small groups and redefining our concepts of community. After decades of atomizing, isolating pressures to "do our own thing," there is a longing for community, for belonging to groups of kindred spirits, for ways of extending our sense of self. We've begun to come together in circles to reconnect with nature, to discuss the need for "meaningful work" that satisfies our souls, and to join in the quest for service that touches the lives of others. The circle is reappearing in our mass culture—we can see it in our architecture, in our logos, in the growing popularity of small-group formats at meetings and conferences. We have begun to remember the importance of nurturing the collective—as we volunteer to sit with a dying person, rebuild our churches burned by arsonists, and save old-growth forests for future generations—*we rejoin the circle of life.*

An Exercise in Stretching the Self

How would your little wisdom circle aid this change in consciousness? Again, it's a practice area for shifting focus from "I" to "We." This shift takes time to happen. After all, we don't always have a "peak experience" when we watch a sunset. But every once in a while the magic happens. A palpable sense of group consciousness comes unexpectedly—in those moments when each member feels a connection to the whole. You'll sense when it happens in your wisdom circle: when other people's stories resonate deeply within you as if they were your own; when you feel a profound sense of communion; when those individual sparks unite and produce the flame of illumination. And when wisdom makes an appearance.

Getting Lost in the Group?

Certain readers may be worried that we're advocating some sort of groupthink or cult mentality in which the individual loses his or her identity. In fact, we're advocating just the opposite. We see the process of development as an individual—finding your own unique sense of meaning in life—enhanced by participation in a wisdom circle. As we'll explain in more detail later, there is strong emphasis on connecting with your own inner guidance and your own expressions of thought and feeling. You learn to do this within the safety and support of a group.

Two questions are ever present in the wisdom circle: "Who is my unique, authentic self?" and "What is the world (group, community, workplace, society) asking of me?" The task becomes one of reconciling the values that serve you and serve the world at the same time. As members gain insight into this reconciliation for themselves, they become stronger individuals, and this newfound strength, in turn, contributes to the integrity and cohesiveness of the group.

Jungian psychiatrist Arthur Colman, who has studied group process for more than twenty years, says:

> *In our full potential we are not separated I's. Each individual is also part of the group, and each group is*

a unity with its own mysteries and its own journey toward wholeness. This . . . collective . . . is not simply a holding ground for individuals. The group, like the individual, is a vital organism in its own right. [This is] a view of wholeness larger than individual wholeness. It is a concept of wholeness based on a Self which includes the cosmos, solar system, Earth, and all the species that inhabit Earth without any notion of a hierarchical preference for humanity. Human consciousness has power, awesome power, and we must develop it as best we can, for it is part of our nature, but this does not give it overarching value in the web of connectedness that is our true context of experience and existence.

THE "CENTER" OF THE CIRCLE

We use the word "center" in a variety of ways. We've spoken of the circle as a place for self-exploration and for developing group cohesion. Finding that "group center" may be a little like walking the labyrinth with its many forward and backward motions. But if you have an overview and know you're heading for the center, it makes the path a lot easier to traverse.

We find it useful to mark the physical center, usually by placing a low table or cloth on the floor, in the middle of the circle. On this table or cloth are objects that remind us that we are gathered in a sacred space. Some circles honor the elements, with fire and water and objects that remind us of our connection to earth and air. The central table (called an altar by some) can also hold objects sacred to the group. One AIDS caregiving group displayed photographs of people who had died from the disease. A circle held in honor of the spring equinox placed a large goose egg in the center. A corporate workteam might put out materials relating to a project they are proud of. The center can also be formed from a contribution by each member of something personally meaningful.

We also use questions to "center" and help focus the group. When well formulated, a question can become an entrance to deeper truth-telling and further bond the group. Ideally, the wisdom circle inquiry is an opportunity to directly and personally uncover some basic insight about ourselves that reminds us of who we truly are, what we truly value. A question that can be used to elicit this insight is: "Tell us something you did you feel proud of. Don't be modest. It can be something you received recognition for or something only you know about." Here is a story one woman told in response:

> *We were living in an apartment in Manhattan and I was a teacher in a middle school. There was a boy named Benji, who was about eight years old, in our building. He was having a hard time learning to read, and his parents weren't able to help him. So a couple of times a week, he and I would meet and read books together. This went on for a couple of years; then his family moved and we lost touch. About ten years later I was startled to see this eighteen-year-old young man walk into my classroom on the last day of school. It was Benji. He said, "Mrs. Glickman, I just graduated from high school today. I wanted to thank you for what you did. If you hadn't helped me learn to read, I know I*

> *would've dropped out of school and never finished. I wanted you to know how much I appreciated that." I never saw him again.*

The circle bore witness to an event that gave meaning to Mrs. Glickman's life. Every person in the circle benefited from the wisdom in her story: how something we may see as a small gesture can reverberate in the life of another person. Most of us simply don't take the time to examine our best moments, nor do we often have the gift of others listening unconditionally. Here is another story:

> *My parents were migrant farmworkers who did their best to raise three kids. There was never an emphasis on going to school. Often I didn't go. When I finally graduated from high school, I enrolled in a junior college and then got into a four-year school. The highest point in my life was when my parents came to my college graduation, and watched their son get a degree and become a teacher.*

Coming up with incisive, truth-demanding questions is a challenge in itself. The wisdom circle format has been, and continues to be, applied in so many different settings that we cannot offer a list of questions tailored to each one. (We offer more help and specific questions in Chapter 13.) Here are two generic questions we suggest:

What unique talents or qualities do I bring to this circle?

Tell us about a watershed event that changed the course of your life.

For organizations we suggest two questions such as these:

What individual experiences have you had that can shed some light on the challenge we as a corporation (nonprofit organization, society, etc.) are facing? Or that provide a vision for our future?

What is the current reality that you wish you could talk about here?

In an essay on strategic questioning, Fran Peavey writes: "Questioning can change your entire life. It can uncover hidden power and stifled dreams inside of you . . . things you may have denied for many years." An example of this kind of question is: *What is something you've always wanted to do but thought was beyond your range of possibility?* Courageous questioning can also further the group process by giving voice to those things that often go unsaid in a group intent on "making nice," or "not rocking the boat." For instance, remarks that are unintentionally racist or sexist often go unchallenged in a casual group.

Many circles will formulate questions that relate to their core issues. Diversity trainers, breast cancer survivors, environmental activists, and AIDS caregivers draw together to meet very specific needs. Other groups choose to focus on spiritual path, racism, or personal relationships and have their own set of questions, as will the single meeting of a wisdom circle prompted by an occasion (Earth Day, a wedding, a conference, or a memorial service). At the honoring or remembrance of a specific individual, a general question might be: "What does each of us wish to say to, or about, this person?"

Some groups that meet on a regular basis allow the topic to surface ad hoc from the needs or concerns of the members. When a group wants to be spontaneous in choosing a topic, here is a way to proceed:

Ask each person to do a two- to three-minute check-in —that is, tell a highlight since the last meeting, or how he or she is feeling now. Participants will more easily be able to focus on the present if they're able to receive validation for whatever preoccupations they've brought with them. The group can choose to use the recent experiences of one or more group members as "grist for the mill." A cautionary note here is that the discussion may stay at the level of soap opera (ongoing reporting of individual incidents and feelings with no sense of self-inquiry or way to learn anything). An effort must be made to allow wisdom to surface about the topics presented. Thus, an "ordinary" topic such as difficulty in a relationship might prompt a discussion on what makes for good and lasting relationships. A concern about money might prompt an inquiry into the challenges of defining and attaining financial well-being.

Guidelines for Questions

- **Choose questions or topics that require thinking (not yes/no questions) and, most important, those that ask participants to *feel* their way into an answer. (For example: *Tell us about a time in your life when you were really scared and how you got through it.*)**
- **Choose questions that require reflection on personal experience, not those that elicit answers based on a**

preconceived belief system. (*When did you first become aware of spirituality as a dimension of your life?*)

- The topic must motivate participants to bring their full emotional, intellectual, and intuitive energies to it. Everyone's deepest desires, needs, and interests must be engaged. The topic must be compelling and "get the juices flowing." (*What do you see as our organization's number one problem, and what can you commit to as part of a solution? What is your personal definition of a successful life?*)
- The topic should carry within it a universal concern—healing wounds, learning about ourselves, rekindling our connection with the Source of Life, or creating a vision for the future. (*What talents do I possess that could be of use in my community?*)
- The topic might elicit stories about connection—our connection to our best selves, to the mission of our group, to others in need, to the Earth. (*How do I contribute daily to the pollution of the Earth? What one habit of mine could I change that would help the environment?*)
- Topics should help people discover the wisdom in their own experience. (*What change of behavior am I most proud of? What was the lesson in a painful situation?*)
- Phrase the question in a way that focuses the response more clearly. "How can I improve my life?" often leads to a laundry list of answers. "What one step of courage can I take now to make my life more fulfilling?" asks participants to focus on a single scenario or direction. This is a much

more useful approach, because it draws more fully on the imagination and is more apt to result in a breakthrough.

In general, you can further the development of group consciousness (the shift from "I" to "We") with questions that focus on one or more of the following:

- **A shared group concern or activity.**
- **An individual concern that is broad enough for each person to address through his or her personal experience.**
- **Universal stories (about rites of passage, spirituality, work relationships, social concerns), as long as everyone keeps speaking from direct experience, and the discussion does not turn into one of abstract philosophy. The combination of a good question and a circle of active listeners makes it easier for each speaker to "plumb the depths."**

Pitfalls

Be careful not to fall into a rut in which the same topics are revisited repeatedly. Have the courage to go beyond the issues that brought you all together, to consider broader concerns that you share in common, such as community needs, organizational challenges, conscious aging, death, and the future you envision for your children.

A wisdom circle depends on *process* as much as content. It's important to keep checking the pulse of the circle from time to time. (*Is this the way we want to choose our focus? Is anybody getting bored with the way we're doing things?*)

Remember to keep a sense of balance in your questions. Invite the positive and joyful into your wisdom circle. Wisdom circles can go beyond serving as self-help or as support groups, dealing with the painful, helpless feelings of their members. Besides those feelings, members can explore anger, fears, and the darker aspects of personality. At the same time, it is vital to realize that our collective wisdom on how to survive and carry on includes accessing the ecstatic parts of life. There is wisdom in remembering that we're here to enjoy life as well as meet the harder challenges it brings.

Spiritual Center

The group also has a spiritual center, which is the sense of supportive community that develops over time and sustains the members between meetings. The spiritual center evolves as group members develop bonds of trust and caring for each other. It reinforces the purposes of the circle as members go about their daily lives.

The People for Peace group in Santa Fe formed during the Gulf War in January 1991. Hundreds of people participated in candlelight vigils and protests. After the war ended, many people continued to meet in circle to address other concerns. The group has set up a dialogue with scientists at Los Alamos on nuclear disarmament, and rallies people for federal hearings about plans for a radioactive dump site. People for Peace has become both a center for political activities and a spiritual hub for the community. Says one member, "At first most of us were scared to face the authorities who led the hearings. But our twice monthly circles for the past six years have given us the strength to speak up and give voice to our convictions."

SUMMARY OF CONSTANT TWO:

Create a collective center. Make a physical center in the room. Mutually agree upon a topic or question that will serve as the central focus of the meeting. A group may choose an issue specific to its needs, or it can allow for topics to surface determined by individual members' needs.

THREE

Ask to Be Informed

We call upon all those who have lived on this earth, our ancestors and our friends, who dreamed the best for future generations, and upon whose lives our lives are built, and with thanksgiving, we call upon them to teach us and show us the way.

—Chinook invocation

Designated circle maker: *I've chosen an opening ritual that will set our intentions in a larger context. I'd like each one of us to call upon a quality of life that we bring to the circle. It could be compassion, clarity, humor—some quality that you know you've worked on in your life. What can we count on from you? As you begin the invocation, please light the small candle in front of you.*

I call the Beauty of the Earth into this circle. May it surround us, and may I bring it into the lives of all those that I touch.

I invite Compassion into our circle tonight. I give gratitude for my work with those who are terminally ill, and the ways it is teaching me to expand my capacity to feel and express compassion.

I call Playfulness into this circle. Help us forgo our seriousness for a bit, lighten up, and have a good time.

I call on the spirit of Integrity into tonight's gathering. Help me bring my actions and behavior into alignment with what I value so that my life can be made more whole.

I call in the children. May we become that village that takes responsibility for all its children.

~

Invoking certain qualities into the circle enlarges our sense of purpose and begins the process of connecting us with our higher selves. When we ask to be informed by these qualities, we are kindling the same energies within ourselves. If someone invokes compassion, she is reminding herself to bring forth that quality when she speaks. And she is reminding the rest of us to do the same. In a larger sense, we are calling on the others to bear witness and assist us in our efforts to manifest the qualities we invoke. The circle maker can suggest we begin by inviting various qualities such as joy, truth-telling, generosity, laughter, openness to change, into the circle. After this "calling in," a qualitative shift in the feeling tone of the group usually occurs. The circle is now graced with a larger awareness of the values you hold and the intentions you carry.

Expanding on "Little Ole Me"

The intention of the third constant is to help us move past our perceived limitations and invite into the circle a more vast and generous part of ourselves. In the circle we hope to go beyond our personas and discover something deeper and more expansive. We intend to go into our hearts—to make a personal connection to soul. We also have the opportunity to grow from what others are willing to share of themselves.

When a small group of people meets over time in a committed manner, hidden wounds may surface. These revelations can be surprising or painful to speakers and listeners alike if they have never experienced such sharing of vulnerability—by themselves or by others—in a group context. It is important for us to ask that the circle be held by a compassionate presence—a reality greater than the sum of all of us present—so that each of us feels safe and supported.

In seeking to fulfill the third constant, we can apply the statement by Thich Nhat Hanh: "I take refuge in the Buddha, the Buddha takes refuge in me." Since the word *buddha* means "waking up" or "the awakened one," this statement refers to one's awakening to certain qualities within oneself. We can rephrase it as, "I take refuge in compassion, compassion takes refuge in me," or, "I take refuge in playfulness, playfulness takes refuge in me." In other words, we can use Nhat Hanh's statement to affirm what we intend and commit to during our time together: to waking up to the quality or qualities that we call into the circle and into our awareness.

The third constant reminds us that we can draw from a larger reserve of energy and wisdom available to us if we but ask. In the book *Desert Wisdom*, Neil Douglas-Klotz reframes familiar passages from the Bible, the Koran, and other sacred writings from the Middle East and breathes fresh life into their message. We're all familiar with "Ask and you shall receive . . . ," which has, perhaps for some, become hackneyed. Listen to this recasting:

> *Ask intensely, like a straight line engraved toward the objects you want; pray with desire, as though you interrogated your own soul about its deepest, most hidden longings, and you will receive expansively, not only what your desire asked, but where the elemental breath led you—love's doorstep, the place where you bear fruit and become part of the universe's power of generation and sympathy.*

We are told many times over in every sacred literature that to align ourselves with the creative power of the universe, all we have to do is ask, pray, invoke, seek, knock . . . *and it shall be opened unto us.* This passage reminds us that we must ask passionately and with clear intention.

You Have to Ask

As Douglas-Klotz points out, the essential wisdom of "Ask and you shall receive . . ." lies in the *asking*. Now, we know that not everything we ask for actually happens. The parents of a child dying from cancer know about intense petitioning. The hopeful Olympic athlete doesn't always have her prayers for a medal answered. But it is more often true that what trips us up lies in our failure to ask, to turn "like a straight line engraved toward the objects" we want. Instead of connecting with our deepest desires, we tend to muddle through our lives, mumbling our wishes and prayers with little vision and conviction.

When we don't ask intensely, that is, when we don't "interrogate our soul" about what it truly needs, we stay at the level of surface fantasy. We often believe that we aren't worthy or capable of embodying our higher selves, or that we haven't grown into them yet. A wisdom circle is an arena for expressing the desire to be our highest selves. We need to be mindful that many qualities of character are hard-won and that what we're asking for may come over time or through difficult and demanding experiences. Constant Three reminds us that we have to ask, and keep on asking from a deep place in our being, for guidance on how to become what we want ourselves to be.

For thousands of years human communities have faithfully transmitted their wisdom from generation to generation through stories and folktales. That legacy has taught its recipients how to survive, what it means to be human, what humankind's purpose is, and what lies beyond the material plane of existence. These same themes come up again and again in wisdom circles—in our desire for fulfilling relationships and meaningful work; our longing to make a contribution to community; our distress about the fate of the Earth; our fears about aging, suffering, and death. The intention to "Ask to be informed" allows us to draw on a larger consciousness as we address these concerns in a fresh way. Calling into the circle positive qualities or inspiring role models helps us create a larger context for our work together. When we invoke "the wisdom of the ancestors," we acknowledge the wisdom of the ages and call upon the richness of our inherited values and stories to aid us in the present.

Asking to Be Informed by the Future

When the Hopi Indians make important decisions, they ask to be guided by their ancestors and by the hopes and needs of the unborn. They consider the wisdom of the last seven generations and then the needs of seven more to come. The Hopis recognize that they are not alone in their decisions but have the welfare of many others to consider. They are aware that their choices have consequences for their children's children—and have an impact upon the future of the world. The intention of this constant is also to envision your place in this vast continuum of human life.

We can ask for wisdom from the future and choose to focus on the "remote consequences" of our actions upon our descendants. We have a direct relationship with those unborn beings who will inhabit this same planet. Is there any question that what we do today will affect the children of tomorrow? A dozen times a day we can make consumer choices that benefit the environment; we can make socially responsible investment choices; we can opt for lifestyle choices that signal voluntary simplicity rather than conspicuous consumption. In a world whose inhabitants are so utterly interdependent, we cannot fully know what impact our daily actions will have on the future, only that they do. We ask that our choices be guided by wisdom that considers their consequences.

Ways to Incorporate This Intention

The circle maker can fulfill the intention of the third constant by following the model provided by the "designated circle maker" at the beginning of this chapter. Ask each person to name a quality they would like to have present in the circle, or one they themselves are willing to exhibit. When we listen deeply, the words of "calling in" or invocation can inspire and enliven us. When we hear people asking for compassion, peace, truth, or healing to enter the circle, those qualities become more real and more present. The circle maker may also want to add this invocation: "We ask to be informed by the wisdom of those who have gone before us, and by the needs of those yet to be born." Through this simple process, we begin to trust that we *can* draw inspiration from our ancestors and from our own closely held values.

Many wisdom circles choose to create the opening ritual from the intention of Constant Three. To help set the tone for the circle, an invocation may be made by one person, or each person may invoke a presence or quality as he or she lights a candle. (Outdoors, each person placing a stone, pinecone, or any object of choice in the center of the circle works well.) Such invocations often begin with: "I would like to invoke the presence of . . ." or "I call in . . ." or "I'd like to ask [X] to join with us. . . ." When you call in something or someone who is important to you personally, such as an ancestor, it is valuable to frame the invocation in such a way that everyone can appreciate the qualities being called into the circle.

I'd like to call my grandmother, Emma, into the circle. I remember her as being the kindest, most understanding person I've ever known.

Learn to trust what comes to mind when it's your turn to offer an invocation. Give yourself time, and see what surfaces from the depths of your heart. This means getting quiet and listening intently to what longs to be spoken *through you.* Learn to trust this process of what we call developing the intuitive voice—a process that enables us to listen to the often faint promptings that arise from within. The more you attend to those promptings, the more you will trust your intuition as it mines for richer veins of wisdom.

A particular kind of invocation calls attention to the location of the circle. In circles based in earth-centered spirituality, it is a custom to call in the four directions—East, South, West, and North. This is a way for participants to anchor themselves squarely on the earth. Because we are defined by our sense of place, by our Earth connection, calling in the four directions signals that we are creating a center, one firmly planted here on holy ground. Traditionally, the East brings vision, the South healing, the West inner wisdom, and the North purpose and meaning to our lives. Each direction is also related to certain colors, animals, and sounds and to one of the four seasons. Calling the directions consecrates our place and our participation in the natural world.

Extending Constant Three into Our Daily Lives

After you are comfortable with the intention of the third constant, "Ask to be informed," you may find yourself invoking a quality or mythic figure on your own—anytime you need inspiration or support. One of the authors routinely invokes the wisdom of the poet Homer before she begins any writing project. Another never embarks on a vision quest without invoking the protection of the Grandmothers. The purpose of this activity can be framed in one of two ways. Either we are calling forth those higher aspects of ourselves, or on other spiritual forces that are indeed available to us.

Seeing ourselves on a continuum with the people in our past and holding the potential of future generations in our trembling hands, as ecologist John Seed says, ennobles our role in the scheme of things. Further, it reminds us that our lives do have purpose, even when that purpose is not clearly discernible. People who regularly use invocations tell us that the proof of their assistance is palpable. You just have to remember to *ask.*

SUMMARY OF CONSTANT THREE:

Ask to be informed by our highest human values such as compassion and truth, by the wisdom of those who have gone before us, and by the needs of those yet to be born. You can also invoke mythical or historical figures who symbolize desired values. One person can speak for the group, or each member can do a personal invocation.

FOUR

Express Gratitude for the Blessings and Teachings of Life

If the only prayer you say in your whole life is "Thank you," that would suffice.

—Meister Eckhart, thirteenth-century monk and mystic

We are grateful for this gathering that offers us nourishment for our souls and brings wisdom to our lives. We feel deep gratitude to the Earth, our home, for sustaining us and teaching us how to live in harmony with all our fellow creatures. Thank you to each individual who has come today to listen and to speak from the heart. Let's acknowledge the joy and strength we receive from this communion.

One of the purest experiences we can have is that of gratitude. Gratitude is a beautiful feeling that links the heart with the head, emotion with thought. When we say "thank you" in a deeply sincere way, we say, in effect, that we are bonded together. The more profound our feelings of gratitude, the greater our desire to respond in the form of acknowledgment, gifts, service, and sacrifice.

Caregivers find their hearts expanded by gratitude. We (the authors) know many volunteers who provide practical and emotional support for people who are ill. They often tell us of the benefits they receive in the process of giving of themselves. As they tend the woundedness of others, their own wounds may also be healed. One especially committed AIDS caregiver in San Francisco has a mantra he repeats when he's helping someone who has particularly horrible symptoms of the disease: "This is my guru in a distressing disguise." Another says she sees Christ in each person she helps. They both are grateful, first for the opportunity to serve, then for the life lessons and spiritual growth they experience through their chosen work. They, and many other caregivers, express how much more they receive than give through their service.

I'll Take a Tuna Salad Sandwich, Please

We are constantly on the receiving end of the gifts of life. Take, for instance, the mundane act of ordering lunch and then receiving your tuna salad sandwich. You probably thank the server, but you are indebted to the person who caught the tuna, to the person who processed it in a factory, to the person who transported it to a warehouse or store, and finally to the person who made your sandwich. To how many people might you offer a "thank you" for doing their part in getting that sandwich to your table?

Then there are the connections we take for granted in the Web of Life. What about the tuna? the green onions? the celery? the wheat? Those were alive and well, living recently on Mother Earth, just as you are now. What gratitude to them for giving up their life energies so that you may continue to live? How many of us take the time to express gratitude for our food, through whose life essence we continue our lives?

Indigenous peoples take the time to offer thanks to the spirits of the animals that have been killed for their gifts of food and clothing. They don't forget to thank the sun and rain for the resurrection of the potato each year. Gratefulness is woven into their every ritual and ceremony.

A single Japanese word captures this sense of indebtedness to everyone and everything that makes a meal possible: *itadakimasu* (pronounced, ee´ ta da kee mas). Saying it at the beginning of a meal honors the sun, the rain, the earthworms, the farmers, the merchants, the cook—everyone and everything that collaborated to bring the meal together. In a word—*itadakimasu*—you are honoring the Source of Life behind it all. You are recognizing that you have been graced by gifts remote and proximate. There is no English equivalent.

Here is a mealtime prayer that may help kindle gratitude in your heart:

I send prayers of gratitude to all the plants and animals that have sacrificed their lives that I might be nourished. May I take this nourishment into my body and in turn give myself to life that others might be nourished. May this food feed the best in me, that I might make beauty and power of my life and serve others as I have been served.

Learning to Say "Thank You"

Gratitude is simple, yet profound. Simple in the sense that we all experience it long before we know the name for it. As infants, we experience hunger and are grateful when food shows up. We're scared and then grateful when a loving person takes us into her or his arms. These basic feelings are the first inklings of gratitude. Later the feeling is connected with a response, usually by some adult who says, "Say 'thank you' for that." We learn to associate the happy feeling of receiving with the necessity of acknowledging the person or source of the gift. Most three-year-olds know enough to say "thank you" when someone gives them something, and they have a rudimentary sense of the meaning of what they're saying. Yet we're told by every wisdom tradition that deeply felt gratitude is also the doorway to mystical insight, to union with the divine. A profound sense of gratitude is always cited as a sine qua non of spiritual development. One of the disciplines in enriching the life of the soul is the simple act, on a daily basis, of expressing gratitude for those important and small things that grace our lives. Here are some offerings we have heard in circle:

I want to say "thank you" to every person in this circle tonight who made it safe for me to tell the story of my divorce. It was hard to admit I was so unconscious and so unaffectionate during those years.

•

I am so blessed by the three children in my life. They are my main teachers. The spiritual readings I've done pale in comparison to what I learn from them each day.

•

I especially want to thank Greg tonight for taking the step to tell me that I was lecturing you all and coming from my head. It may take awhile, but I'll find that heartspace yet. Bear with me. I know it's there.

•

Thank you from the bottom of my heart to each person in this circle for holding onto the mission of this agency. That's what integrity is all about.

The fourth constant is seemingly the easiest of all to learn, which makes its power to reshape our relationships all the more sublime. Expressing gratitude is deceptively simple, for it is something we've been doing all our lives. For that very reason, it can easily become perfunctory and shallow. Weaving a deep sense of gratitude into the fabric of our everyday awareness takes a lifetime.

The payoff for expressing gratitude in a wisdom circle is immediate. When you allow feelings of gratefulness to well up inside and communicate them aloud, an undeniably positive feeling pervades the group. Elizabeth Roberts, in her wonderful book *Earth Prayers*, says that "at the heart of gratefulness, we also find an expression of belonging. When we say 'Thank you' we're really saying 'We belong together.'" We are acknowledging our interdependence.

Saying "thank you" to someone is, in effect, saying, "I am part of you, you are part of me." And who among us doesn't want to belong to something larger than our finite selves?

Gratitude to Whom?

When we express a general feeling of gratitude for the blessings and teachings of life, to whom are we speaking? Since each person brings his or her own spirit of inquiry into the circle, each one may have a different way of identifying the Source of Life. In the circle we often leave the "to whom" ambiguous and use phrases such as "Gratitude to Life for . . ." or "I am grateful for. . . ." In this book we often use the term "Source of Life" to include the many different forms of transpersonal reality. It is in the spirit of a wisdom circle to honor *all* expressions of that sentiment, however named.

There are so many ways to fulfill the fourth constant in a wisdom circle that it may be easy to overlook or forget the importance of it. Gratitude can be expressed by each person in a round, to anyone and for anything he or she chooses. The circle maker can suggest that the group offer gratitude for a specific gift, such as the company of kindred spirits. This can be done in silence, by each person speaking in turn, or by one person speaking for the whole group.

An effective way to end a wisdom circle is to make the closing ritual an outpouring of gratitude for whatever has been offered in the circle. Each person can express it in his or her own words.

- *I want to thank everyone here for their wisdom and for taking the risk of expressing deeply personal feelings.*

- *Gratitude for letting me know that I'm not alone in my concern for the future of our children.*
- *I want to thank my dear grandfather, who I invoked in the beginning of the circle for his courage to come to this country and start a new life. My life has been very blessed as a result of his vision.*

The important point is that here again, just as with the three preceding constants, we are embedding our individual lives in a larger context. Gratitude evokes a feeling of reverence and bonds the members of a group more closely together. It's yet another pathway for getting from "I" to "We." Here are two responses to the question, "What are you grateful for?"

> *I began work as a mental health counselor for people with the HIV virus about a year ago. Since then I've seen a lot of gay men and hear over and over their stories about how painful it is to be estranged from your family—some for most of their lives—because their parents could not accept the fact that they were homosexual. I am so grateful to those men for opening me up and helping me to understand that kind of pain. I have a two-and-a-half-year-old son and before I started this work, I used to envision him growing up, getting married, having children of his own. Never once did I consider the possibility that he might be gay. I know now that I will love him and support him in whatever sexual orientation he chooses.*

•

My two-year-old son had a cardiac arrest in November and went into a coma. I brought him home in December and rocked him for eight to fifteen hours a day, holding him, begging for a miracle. My group, called the Mother's Circle, gathered together, and each brought me a flower and a bead to represent something positive about me they wanted me to remember. I took the beads and made another powerful circle—a necklace that sustained me through that fog of pain. My baby died in May, and for many months afterward I was unable to face leaving the house unless I was wearing my "Friend" necklace for strength. There are no words for how grateful I am to my circle for their support during that time.

Extending Gratitude into Our Daily Lives

Let gratitude become a "habit of the heart." You'll discover that this simple practice can reverberate powerfully in your life. As you act upon this constant within and then outside of your wisdom circle, you'll remember it more and more often. You'll become more conscious of that feeling of gratefulness welling up in your heart when you see a loved one, smell a flower, hear a moving piece of music. You'll find gratitude a healing balm during times of grief, anger, self-pity, and loneliness, when dark times make us feel so cut off, so isolated in our inner world. The fuller our gratitude, the less room there is for depleting negative emotions. Gratitude connects; it reminds us that we are part of something larger. It puts us heartfully in touch with other people and with the Web of Life. With practice, you may even find yourself able to appreciate the lessons from the harsher teachers of life—the losses, the pain, and the failures. With practice, you will discover more and more reasons to be grateful, as Gunilla Norris does in her lovely meditation in *Being Home*:

This morning as I put my feet on the floor
let me remember how many thousands of years
it took for this act to be possible—
the slow and painstaking development
so that a human creature could rise,
could stand on two feet, and then walk.

SUMMARY OF CONSTANT FOUR:

Express gratitude for the blessings and teachings of life. Acknowledge and honor our interdependence with everything in the Web of Life. In silence, or by taking turns, give thanks for those people and those things great and small whose gifts enrich and nourish you.

FIVE

Create a Safe Container for Full Participation and Deep Truth-Telling

The moment we cease to hold each other,
the moment we break faith with one another,
the sea engulfs us and the light goes out.

—James Baldwin,
as quoted in Loneliness and Love *by Clark E. Moustakas*

This circle is a home where we feel known, trusted, and valued. It is a safe container where we can draw upon our innate capacities for wisdom, compassion, and self-healing. We humans have depended on such capacities for millennia. We have also depended on each other for a sense of sanctuary. In the circle, each of us can reveal our fears, show our vulnerabilities, and give voice to our dreams. A safe space where we can begin a "foolish project" like learning to live together in harmony. It's time to begin a "foolish project."

CREATE A SAFE CONTAINER

We all long to feel safe and protected from harm. Yet in our world has physical safety become a luxury only a few can afford? Can you go on an airplane, walk into a government building, go to the Olympics, even sleep in your own bedroom if you live in a drug-dealing neighborhood, and feel physically safe? Each day the news reminds us that our bodies are fragile targets for random violence. What about emotional safety? How often are we in situations where we can "let our hair down" and reveal deep feelings? Where can we put aside the masks of personality, give up that false front of being "okay"? How often do you allow your authentic self to engage in conversation? Would you even know its texture and voice? Authenticity is revealed through our eyes, our posture, and our voice and by the words we choose when we speak from the heart. We may reveal our authentic selves only when it feels safe to do so.

Billions of times a day around the world, one person asks another: "How are you?" And 90 percent of the time the other person responds, "fine." Are we all so fine? Or do we need to hide our true state of mind or health because we don't feel the relationship warrants an authentic response? Or because there's not enough time to "get into it"? Rare is the adult who shows up authentically—consistently. One is usually regarded as a crazy fool or a saint. Authenticity is one of the greatest challenges we face in life. It means not playing at roles, but being genuine and truthful. We are experienced as authentic by others when we are willing to self-disclose and create two-way intimacies with every other member of the circle.

A wisdom circle is a place where your authentic self is encouraged to show up—not just encouraged, but explicitly invited and esteemed to show up in a way that honors your life experiences. You want to be seen for your uniqueness, for the pains you've suffered, and for the expansive capacity you have for experiencing beauty and joy. A wisdom circle is a place where your authentic self is the invited guest.

The role of circle maker was rotating among the eight members of the group, and each person was encouraged to draw from their ethnic heritage as part of designing the opening ritual. When Miriam was asked if she would take on the role at the next meeting, she said she was reluctant because she was afraid the group would think her "too Jewish." After members reminded her that diversity was one of the principal concerns of the group, Miriam laughingly agreed to do it. During her opening ritual, Miriam lit candles, said Hebrew prayers, and explained the ritual of Shabat. Everyone thanked her warmly for the introduction to that beautiful form and said kiddingly they thought she was "just Jewish enough." During the circle she admitted that she'd only recently reembraced Judaism, and she wasn't entirely comfortable with putting herself out as being recommitted to her religion.

Miriam demonstrated that truth-telling is a major component of being authentic. When she honestly asked herself why she had been uncomfortable doing the ritual, she discovered the source of her anxiety was not "out there" in the group, but within herself.

THE BUILT-IN SAFETY DEVICES

Just as you pay close attention to the instructions about oxygen masks and seat flotation cushions the first few times you fly on an airplane, it is good to know five safety devices that are built into a wisdom circle:

1. **The creation of sacred space**
2. **The intention to listen and speak from the heart**
3. **The talking object**
4. **The choice to remain silent**
5. **The commitment to confidentiality**

These are such powerful safety elements that we've seen groups of strangers walk into sterile hotel meeting rooms and willingly reveal things to each other in circle that they had not said to loved ones in years, if ever.

When we're in a temple, a church, a mosque, or other sacred place, we don't expect to be verbally attacked, embarrassed, or made fun of in a disrespectful way. A wisdom circle is also a sacred place that offers us the promise that we will be treated with respect, that we are and will be "safe." This safety is crucial to the emergence of deep truth-telling. In a circle, we can allow ourselves to be truly seen and can stop trying to "look good" to others.

Twenty-five men with drums sat in a circle on the floor around an altar with candles at a residential drug-recovery program. Some of the men had just come from prison; others were mandated by the courts to enter the program as a condition of probation. After drumming together for about thirty minutes, the ques-

tion was raised: "Can you remember that special place in nature where you could be alone and safe, and dream your dreams when you were a child?" Each man answered as the talking stick came to him. There were memories of fishing trips with Dad, a tree house, a hiding place in the tall grass. Some stories included tearful memories of a momentary refuge from rage and abuse. For most, if not all, of these men, this circle was the first time it had ever been safe to show feelings of vulnerability in the company of other men.

Imagine the pain of going to your grave with the feeling of never having been truly seen or heard by anyone. People have commented after a wisdom circle that they don't remember having been "listened to" so intently in their entire lives. In an ongoing circle, as a member feels more trust, she may choose to reveal more of a painful past, or an anxious present circumstance. When personal feelings are witnessed by others, healing can begin. Not only for the one who speaks, but for those who listen. Your words may resonate with others, and some new truth may surface that is of use to them—all because you took the risk to speak authentically.

This story may make me look a little naïve, but I think there's a message in it. I had bad arthritis in my fingers, and the doctors wanted to operate and replace some knuckles. My daughter was going to visit the Lourdes shrine in France, and I asked her to bring back some of the holy water. She did, and I used it sparingly for six months, rubbing it on my fingers. The arthritis disappeared. After that my daughter told me: "Mom, the water I brought back from Lourdes spilled all over my suitcase. I didn't want to disappoint you so I gave you some tap water." I learned about my own healing powers.

This woman took the risk of looking like a fool in telling her truth. We learn to trust each other with our heartfelt stories and experiences. Over time, we see the circle as a place where vulnerable feelings will be honored and accepted, where fragile insights can be shared, where we can risk looking foolish or stand up for ourselves in a way we never have before.

I remember a woman who was very shy and had never spoken in circle who suddenly started dancing. She felt the impulse to express what she was feeling through movement. I knew she'd moved way past the person she thought she could be in public. When one person stretches their sense of what they're capable of, it stretches everyone in the group. Her spontaneity was a gift to all of us.

•

I was in circle with other hospice professionals. I took a risk in saying that I regretted not being able to express my feelings to some of my clients before they died. I didn't tell them how deeply I cared about them, how grateful I was to know them, or how much they had taught me. I don't talk easily about my inadequacies, but the safety and love of that particular circle allowed me to.

Confidentiality is of the utmost importance. In order to feel safe, you must feel certain that anything you say will not be taken outside the circle. All circle members must commit to honoring this trust. This means not revealing what's said in the circle to anyone who's not a member of it, even to a spouse or partner. Any breaching of this trust undermines the circle because members may feel betrayed and become less willing to share deeply and fully. A person can be badly hurt when confidentiality is broken, and the breach can destroy the group.

The Talking Stick

We strongly suggest using a "talking stick" or other symbolic object in the early years of your wisdom circle. It gives the person holding it the right to speak without interruption. Any object that has meaning for the members can be used—a stick, a rock from someone's garden, a sacred text, a flower that represents what may be blossoming in the group, a rattle, a photograph. The object teaches us how to listen by reminding us to focus on the speaker and the speaker's search for his or her authentic voice. We may not agree with everything another says, but we honor the person's right to say it. The talking stick or object empowers the person to speak, and it empowers the rest of us to listen. After long practice with the stick, some groups find they have internalized the pacing of a wisdom circle so well that they don't need to use a physical object very often. But the ability to do without the stick only comes after much practice. If members forgo use of the stick too soon, the atmosphere becomes one of an ordinary discussion group.

People who are reticent or shy in groups are especially empowered by the use of a talking object. So many times we've witnessed people considered "the quiet ones" speak their truths without fear simply because they've been given the time to collect their thoughts with no interruptions. When you take a few moments to simply hold the talking stick, you may discover a feeling or thought that you weren't previously aware of. Free to let a longer silence enter the circle, you can also take that opportunity to go more deeply into yourself. People who are not ready to speak may simply hold the stick and then pass it on. They can do this until they are ready to take the risk of speaking from the heart.

On the other hand, there are those for whom speech comes easily—too easily. They add drama, humor, and wit to whatever they're saying. They speak to entertain, and to impress. It may be more difficult for such people to speak authentically. The slower pace of the circle, mandated by having to pass the talking object, teaches people who are facile with words to slow down, choose their words carefully, and say things simply and to the point. Speaking in circle is not about making an impression. It's about making an expression of personal truths. It's about "getting real."

There are two customary ways to pass a stick in a wisdom circle. One is to keep the stick in the center; the person wishing to speak picks it up and then returns it to the middle when he or she is done. If the group is large, or getting up and down is difficult for some people, then the stick can pass clockwise around the circle. We caution against succumbing to the "tyranny of the stick." When it comes to you, you are under no obligation to speak. You can pass it on, hold it awhile and pass it on, or choose to speak.

All you need to do to fully participate in a wisdom circle is to listen compassionately. Again, there is no requirement to speak. The choice to remain silent is another assurance that you can reveal yourself at a pace you are comfortable with and when you feel ready. An often-heard comment in a wisdom circle is: "I'm glad I waited to hear others before I spoke. Listening to them brought things to mind and changed what I wanted to say."

What if someone holds the stick so long that other members of the circle get irritated? A gentle reminder to the long-winded person may be enough, but sometimes this can be a difficult issue. When a person first experiences the undivided attention of others, it can be a heady experience. He or she may be largely unaware of the passing of time or of the fact that others, too, have a need to speak. Some people get at their deeper truths by rambling around in a free-associative fashion to allow them to surface, and this searching can take a long time.

Initially, the circle needs to be tolerant of this style of expression. However, if the same person holds the stick for a long time every time, there may need to be some limits set. Before a topic is addressed, members can reach consensus about how much time will be spent on the round. Then everyone can roughly estimate how much time he or she has to speak, which keeps each member in the ballpark. Another solution is to designate a monitor who can gently ring a chime when the speaker's time is up. (Of course, if the speaker is in the middle of delving into a powerful issue, the monitor needs to use discretion.)

No Cross-Talk or Advice Giving Unless Solicited

It is customary in the wisdom circle format to have no cross-talking while someone is holding the talking stick, *unless that person solicits feedback from another person or from the group*. Each individual is responsible simply to bear witness to each other's words. By doing so, members feel protected—they know no one will try to "rescue" them or offer advice. Often it is simply enough to tell your story, to offer your feelings and insights to the group. You may not want to be told what you need to learn from those feelings or what step to take next. You may also be bowled over by your own words and need a moment of silence. Holding the stick for a few moments after you finish creates that silence. If someone asks for feedback, we encourage others to speak from their own experience rather than saying, "You ought to . . ." or "You should. . . ."

Your group may modify the meeting's format to suit its needs. Sometimes an open discussion is called for on some aspect of the group's plans, or a report has to be given. Members of the Women's Forest Sanctuary wisdom circle decided to spend an hour in an open meeting and then allocate an hour for a wisdom circle. A health-care group decided to have their wisdom circle first and then participate in what was called "out-of-circle dialogue," which was an open discussion of other issues they needed to attend to and comments on the process of the circle itself.

Our experience has been that wisdom circles of long duration (over two years) can successfully maintain the pace of the talking object without always using one. It is usually the more extroverted members who suggest putting aside the stick. As noted earlier, when use of the stick is abandoned prematurely, it doesn't take long for the circle to lose its center and become an ordinary discussion group with someone jumping in nine-tenths of a second after another person finishes. Lost are the feeling of sacred space and the sense of safety required for deep truth-telling.

SUPERSAFE?

Finally, we have to ask the question, "How safe should a wisdom circle be?" So safe that only very nice, polite things are ever said? So safe that no one is ever offended, made angry, or rocked off center? No, not that safe. The issue of safety has more to do with sustaining a loving, supportive environment in which to take risks of self-discovery and self-revelation. A group that stays superficial never establishes a real sense of safety.

"Nice" people who don't want in any way to tread on each other's sensitivities, or raise uncomfortable issues, or engage in deep truth-telling, don't need a wisdom circle. They could just as easily play Scrabble or watch a baseball game together, both pretty low-risk activities. A wisdom circle has a different set of intentions: to set up the conditions for our collective wisdom to emerge and to practice compassion for each other so that our wisdom and compassion become central to how we engage each other and people in the world at large. To do that, we have to create a sense of communion, not just polite rapport. We have to discover our rough edges with one other, acknowledge them, and find ways of reconciling (not suppressing or dismissing) our many differences.

Ideally, a wisdom circle is a safe place to push the edges of our awareness. You may address an issue that hits so close to home that one or more people may feel anywhere from uncomfortable to fearful to downright angry. Or, despite all the emphasis on speaking and listening from the heart and rules on advice giving, something unkind or inappropriate is said to another participant. Such things happen, especially as group members try to get more "real" with each other.

At this point, it's important to distinguish between *honesty*, which may be accurate but needlessly hurtful, and *truth-telling*, which considers the larger context and other people's vulnerability and state of mind. The main thing to remember is that we are here primarily to be compassionate witnesses, which means we choose words with care that are not meant to wound or label people.

Although it may not feel good at the time, a painful remark or an angry exchange can also be used to "make medicine," that is, to explore what transpired and to work toward healing a rift between two or more members. However, some ruptures cannot be mended, in which case someone drops out of the group, or the group splits, with people taking sides. (We will go into more detail on skillful ways of handling difficulties in Chapter 15.) Such divisiveness, so prevalent in the world around us, can appear in the microcosm of the circle. If we cannot work out our differences and learn to respect each other in the context of a friendly group, how can we possibly resolve the chasms between us based on race, gender, ethnicity, sexual orientation, class, and religion that exist in the larger society? A wisdom circle is a practice arena that teaches us tolerance for other views and life expressions.

What other situations can cause a wisdom circle to feel

unsafe? What if my spouse, boss, or child is present? How can I be truthful, how can I show weakness or vulnerability? It is generally not a good idea to be in a circle with people you feel you have to hide significant parts of yourself from. Charlie [Garfield] once led a wisdom circle for the staff of an overstressed social service agency and felt that some people were being unusually reticent. The group was a mix of managers and their employees, and since the topic was "What's going on here that hinders you from doing your best work?" some people were understandably holding back. It is possible to gather people who are unequal in power or position, or who are at odds with one another, or who are even diametrically opposed to one another, in the same wisdom circle. But success in doing so requires experience with the process of the circle, a clear idea of the common goals of the group, and a commitment to abide by the Ten Constants.

This caution does not preclude the use of wisdom circles in families or classrooms or in other arenas in which "authority figures" are present. In their book *The Way of Council*, Jack Zimmerman and Virginia Coyle detail how "council" (whose purposes are similar to those of wisdom circles) has been used very successfully in schools and within families. We recommend their book for applications in those areas.

The following is a segment from an essay written by a junior high school student whose teacher introduced her class to the wisdom circle:

> *I used to think that the circle was some stupid hippie thing. Then last week, just before vacation, we did a circle where the question was: who are you sad that you can't be with at Christmas. Someone lit the flame of*

truth in the middle. I started to cry when Barbara talked about her father being dead. I didn't know that and I thought we were good friends. I learned that circle is a place where you can say anything and know that the other kids won't laugh at you. You can cry and it won't matter. For 45 minutes we can bring our thoughts and dreams into a circle of kids. It doesn't matter what color you are, your age, your sex, or your background, we are all equal and the circle tells me that we can *live in a never ending circle of love, happiness and peace.*

Here is an exercise to gauge your circle's level of safety. If one of the following questions were the focus of your wisdom circle, you would need a few minutes of silence to gather your thoughts and feelings. Would you speak, or would you pass the talking stick? How would you respond?

- **Describe one of the most important things you have learned in life so far.**
- **How is life for the person who gets up every morning feeling part of the "majority" culture, different from life for the person who feels stereotyped or devalued by the majority culture? Which person do you identify with?**
- **Are you holding any anger toward anyone in this circle? Why?**
- **What do you think will happen to you after you die?**
- **What holds you back from living out your full creativity?**

SUMMARY OF CONSTANT FIVE:

Create a container for full participation and deep truth-telling. Allow each person to speak without interruption or cross-talk. Pass the talking stick (or any object that has symbolic significance) around the circle, until everyone has the opportunity to participate. Respect a member's right to silence. Keep everything confidential.

SIX

Listen from the Heart

When we are seen by the heart we are seen for who we are. We are valued in our uniqueness by those who are able to see us in this way and we become able to know and value ourselves.

—*Rachel Naomi Remen,*
Kitchen Table Wisdom

Let's remember that the talking stick or stone serves the listeners as much as it does the speaker. It teaches us how to listen—respectfully, with full attention. It asks us to quiet the inner voice, the one that tends to evaluate, compare, disagree, and judge. It reminds us that we are each trying to speak from the heart as best we can. At any moment, something may be said that is exactly what we need to hear—and it may surprise us.

I come to the wisdom circle with this hope: Let me see the world through your eyes, hear the world as you hear it. Let us teach each other, support each other, inspire each other, and heal each other. Let us make visible to ourselves, and then to the world, how much we care.

Consider what stories you might hear in the following wisdom circles:

- *It's the first Saturday of spring, and a group of twelve people are gathered in a wisdom circle to honor cycles and new beginnings. Each person speaks to a cycle they count on for their renewal—a yearly vacation, the menstrual cycle, the annual nesting activities of mourning doves on the back porch. When the talking stick comes to the eight-year-old, he says the cycle he's interested in right now is the return of the comet, Hyakutake.*
- *Six physicians all serving at a public hospital in a major city recount a moment when they each received a critical insight about how to be a doctor, from a patient.*
- *Eight people on a work team at a book publishing company ask, "Which book of the fifteen we've worked on together in the past year are you most proud of, and why?"*
- *A group of seven parents of disabled children answer the question: "What are your toughest moments, and how do you get through them?"*
- *A group of twelve eco-activists address the question: "When have you been most tempted to resort to violence in support of your cause? What prevented you from doing that?"*

- *A group of ten women (all with professional careers) calling themselves the Suburban Goddess Network respond to the question, "What step of courage can you take at this time to make your life more fulfilling?"*
- *Six North American children sit in a circle with six children from India to explore the question, "How are we the same, and how are we different?"*
- *Thirty-five women sit in a circle on the floor, telling each other what their greatest challenge is right now. Seven of them say it is the lingering effects of having been sexually abused by their fathers.*

By listening from the heart, we collect the wisdom of circle members in the form of stories imbued with expression of feelings. Listening is the *primary* activity of a wisdom circle; it is the only thing you need to do to be a fully participating member. It requires us to walk into the emotional life of the person speaking, to share their hopes and fears as fully as we can. When we listen from the heart, we are giving ourselves heart to heart. As we grow in this capacity, we find ourselves able to hear the deeper messages, the universal themes that resound in all of our lives. Over time, we get better at discerning the wisdom hidden in the rough articulations. And best of all, we expand our capacity for unconditional love.

Listening as Hospitality

Listening from the heart means you give a "Welcome" sign to the speaker, who's wondering whether to trust you with his or her thoughts and feelings. Through your respectful silence, eye contact, body posture, and attentiveness, you signal that you are listening with empathy. Such heartfelt concentration creates a space in which each member of the circle can speak freely, feeling like an invited guest.

Such "hospitality" requires the willingness and ability to see life through another's eyes. Learning to listen with such deep empathy is no easy task. Most of us have not learned how to do this. Psychotherapists, counselors, spiritual advisers, social workers, and other professionals spend years perfecting this capacity. Psychologist Carl Rogers described empathic listening as follows:

> *To be with another in this way means that for the time being you lay aside the views and values you hold for yourself in order to enter another's world without prejudice. In some sense it means that you lay aside your self and this can only be done by a person who is secure enough in himself that he knows he will not get lost in what may turn out to be the strange or bizarre world of the other, and can comfortably return to his own world when he chooses.*

Another way of understanding this deep form of communication comes from Dr. Milton Greenblatt and his colleagues at Harvard University Medical School. They recorded the heart rates of patients and their psychiatrists. When the patient's heart rate increased, usually in reporting anxiety-provoking experiences, so did the psychiatrist's. When the patient's heart rate slowed down, the doctor's heart slowed down as well. Though both parties were unaware of their heart rates, their rates were in synch when they felt they were communicating with each other. Experienced bodywork therapists also report that a strong rapport with clients produces a similar entrainment.

This kind of physical bonding can occur in circle when participants listen from the heart. There is a biological as well as spiritual basis for heart-to-heart communication. We feel our hearts beating rapidly when we listen to stories of desperate circumstances. We have felt our hearts sink, as if crushed by a heavy weight, when we listen to tales of pain or loss. By allowing each other's sadness, confusion, excitement, and happiness to resound within us, we build the solidarity of the circle.

This Is Not about "Fixing"

We invite many emotions to a wisdom circle, including fear and anger and those associated with grief, loss, and abuse. Yet we resist our inclination to offer advice or rescue the hurting person in some way. A wisdom circle is not a psychotherapy or counseling session, although being listened to empathically can have a strong healing effect on the speaker.

We need to remind ourselves that we are gathered in this particular format to share our truths—not to "fix" each other. As we bear witness, we help the speaker make sense of her own life, find her own answers, know her own strength. Silent witnessing allows the speaker to dig deeper and recognize her own unique journey. As she plumbs deeper and deeper into her own life story, she can learn from the obstacles she's encountered. Just the very act of feeling heard and understood gives the speaker added hope and strength.

When stories of family dysfunction are being told, stories of neglect, violence, and abuse, a listener may have as much difficulty bearing witness as the speaker has in telling her or his tale. It is important that we honor the courage required to speak the unspeakable and not interfere with the process, even if it makes us feel uncomfortable. If a listener intervenes and stops the process, the speaker retreats from self-disclosure, holding his pain and guilt. Or the speaker may think that his story is "too much" for the group and feel compelled to take care of the listeners' feelings. An opportunity for healing is then postponed or lost.

The Drunken Monkey

Minding our own minds is surely the biggest challenge in fulfilling the intention of the sixth constant. The Hindus refer to the mind as a drunken monkey, swinging wildly from tree to tree. The speaker's comments may elicit strong emotional reactions in us and set our minds reeling. We may find what he or she is saying diametrically opposed to our perception of the way things work. An individual's ethnic background, gender, socioeconomic class, or age may conjure up long-held stereotypes that affect our judgment of that person's worth or credibility. Or we may find our attention drifting when it's hard to connect the speaker's story to our own lives.

Listening from the heart tests our emotional, psychological, and spiritual resources. It asks us to find that center-point of pure receiving, where we relax our opinions and our dearly held assumptions to make room for new ideas and where we can show a greater degree of lovingkindness. Then perhaps, yes! that spark of wisdom may appear.

I have made it a practice when I hear somebody saying something I don't particularly like, to say to myself:

> *"And that attitude also lives in me." So I feel that has expanded my heart quite a bit. It's a process of reclaiming my own shadow, and it's required me to get bigger inside in order to do that, and I'm committed to that "internal bigness."*

> *I've spent the better part of my adult life dealing with a judgmental nature. That certainly starts with judging myself, and extends to lots of other people and situations. In a wisdom circle, I'm so conscious of being in the moment, of listening with an open heart, of trying to hear the underlying messages, of taking people at their best, thinking they're doing the best they can—that the judgmental part of me fades away.*

It may take more than a few circles to learn how to suspend our judgments, biases, and prejudices, for we have to create the same kind of space that meditation requires. We begin by clearing the mind's chatter, which means not rehearsing replies, not making comparisons, and shrugging off the voices in your head that say, "She's really off the wall," or "I wish he'd get his thinking together," or "I'm glad I've resolved that problem in *my* life."

We like to think of a wisdom circle as a form of group meditative practice, with the speaker the object of our meditation. Again, this is a learned skill, just like solo meditation. We assume an attitude of mindfulness, attending to the speaker's words as they arise in our own awareness. Legendary family therapist Virginia Satir said she honed her listening skills as a social worker, interviewing delinquent teenagers who had committed horrible crimes. One young man had killed both his parents in a rage. It was her role to listen to his story. What does it take to listen from the heart to a person who has murdered someone? Who has sexually abused a child? Who has conned elderly people out of their life savings? Listening to such people does not mean we condone or excuse such behavior, but it does mean having to cope with a vortex of thoughts and emotions: from anger and disgust to acceptance and understanding. It does mean finding the Christ, the Buddha nature, the soul, the worthiness within someone who has done something despicable. You will probably seldom encounter anything so challenging within your wisdom circle. But cultivating this generosity of heart is something we can all aspire to.

The Payoff Is Tremendous

Being listened to unconditionally has healing properties. We have each seen people blossom in a wisdom circle who previously felt they had never really been listened to in their entire lives. They say the experience has given them hope, dignity, and a sense of self-worth they never had access to before. When the circle concentrates intently on our stories of joy and sorrow, we come to trust our inner world. We learn that our narratives are worthwhile and may be offered as a gift to others.

To varying degrees, we all feel unheard. Where do you get to tell your important life stories again and again until *you* understand them? To your family? To your best friends? They may balk after hearing the same story several times. The members of your wisdom circle, however, understand that repetition of important stories is crucial to learning their life lessons. For individuals who are grieving, the telling and retelling of the story of the loss and its pain are vital aspects of their healing journey.

The listener, too, develops greater emotional resilience. One AIDS caregiver said that his capacity for listening grounded him so that he was not "blown out of the water" by stories about excruciating symptoms and medical treatments. Compassionate listening also helps us clear away the baggage of stereotypes.

> *I had never known anyone who used intravenous drugs before I met Leo in a caregivers circle. I had a picture of "those IV drug users," but Leo didn't fit it. He looked clean-cut and was very articulate. After I heard his story about growing up in the casinos of Atlantic City and the emotional abuse he had endured, my heart opened to him. It was one of those moments when you say to yourself, "There but for the grace of God, go I." Leo and I have stayed in touch, and I have a lot of respect for him.*

When we listen from the heart, we can empty ourselves of long-held prejudices and make the speaker's interests our own. As a consequence, we receive the gift of seeing through the eyes of another and perhaps that of entering a new world we have had no access to. Such stories can germinate like seeds in our hearts and bear fruit throughout our lives.

The sixth constant is a path to greater spiritual awareness. Listening from the heart is a deep meditative practice that opens up your awareness to increasingly subtle levels of communication. You become better at discerning those nuggets of wisdom hidden in everyday speech. You learn how to find the emotional thread when the speaker gets lost in her own labyrinth—when she follows a stream of consciousness that leads back to kindergarten and then to her trip to New York for the first time and then to her grandmother's house. You also learn to hear the cries of pain and hope under the bare "facts" of a story told without emotion. Most important, you grow to be more in touch with your own "still small voice within." You will also learn to appreciate nonverbal cues, such as tone of voice and body posture. In addition, your capacity for intuition will expand.

There is an instructive parable about an opinionated Englishman who went to visit a Zen master. The teacher fills the visitor's tea cup until it is overflowing all over the ground. "Why are you doing that?" the Englishman finally asks. The teacher replies: "This cup is like your mind, too full for anything new to enter." Listening from the heart empties our minds so new levels of awareness can gain admittance.

Cultural Considerations

If your life is working relatively well, listening from the heart may be easier for you than it is for people who have been marginalized by society. In the words of psychiatrist Arnold Mindell, "As long as you're not feeling oppressed, it's easy to listen. . . . Expecting someone who has been marginalized to be the listener can be oppressive and irritating to that person." With a great deal of conscious work, it is possible to hold a wisdom circle that mixes people of different subcultures that have had little contact with one another. Remember that those of us who have been badly hurt by racism, sexism, homophobia, or other forms of discrimination will often be wary of presumed status differences. Some of us may hold smoldering angers and attitudes hardened by social injustices. These don't magically disappear when the circle opens. If you are fortunate enough to have a cross-cultural circle, you will have the added benefit of learning from people whose life experiences have been very different from your own, although everyone will probably have to work harder at listening in order to hear what's really being said.

The question, "Why can't we all be friends?" from white people to people of color is often answered by people of color with, "We can, when I can bring all of who I am and my day-to-day realities into the relationship."

> *I'm sitting in this circle as a Chicano, and I'm very aware of that. I know this circle is meant to foster better understanding among people of different races, but I see a majority of white people, with one African American and two other Latinos. You ask us to come into your organizations, attend your conferences, meet with you in this church, which has a predominately white congregation, so we can "communicate" better. Why don't you come to a Chicano conference, or to my church? I'm tired of being asked to come into white territory in order to improve "race relations." I'd like you to come into my world, then maybe we can create some* common *territory.*

Collective Benefit

How can we tell when focused self-concern begins to move toward empathy and compassion for others? As each person speaks, another life lesson is shared. When I listen attentively, I can assimilate this lesson. It can become part of my inner reality. If I then embrace it as *my* idea, my joy, my pain, my fear, my surprise, my life lesson, then something I may count on as *my* learning is born within *me*. My internal guidance is broadened, refined, and enriched. "You and I" become "we." The result is that the concerns of the members become *my own*.

I transcend the rigid separation between myself and another person. My tight personal boundary blurs, as happens in lovemaking. It's what Buddhist scholar Joanna Macy calls "the greening of the self," whereby our narrow sense of self is "replaced by wider constructs of self-interest, by the eco-self," by our identification with other beings and with the life of the planet. Psychiatrist Arthur Colman explains it this way:

> *We functionally define individuation as a process of becoming fully and wholly oneself without compromise to society, [yet] there is a sense [that] as an individual grows in that direction, he or she becomes more conscious and involved with the surrounding world.*
>
> *This is a model of an individuated person: someone who serves himself or herself and the group from a place of self-knowledge. Without knowledge and acceptance of the group as part and parcel of one's identity, there is no service, and no individuation.*

Colman fully understands that when there is no strongly developed "I," mobs and cults begin to flourish. Yet he makes a case for the necessity of a person developing in two fundamental ways: as an individual and as a member of the collective. He says that "individuation in its fullest sense must finally include group consciousness or risk being synonymous with narcissistic individualism." He goes on to state: "It is our penchant for narrowly defined individuality in opposition to the collective that constricts us, prevents us from grasping the whole, stops us short of the fullness of individuation."

In more poetic terms, author James Baldwin observes: "The moment we cease to hold each other, the moment we break faith with one another, the sea engulfs us and the light goes out."

A wisdom circle, then, is a place where "We" becomes embedded in "I" and where "I" becomes embedded in "We." This interpenetration of self and other relates not only to people's spiritual practice. It has major implications for how society must address social, economic, and environmental challenges. *We must do it together.* Many traditional spiritual paths, many disciplines for transcending from individual to universal consciousness exist. Perhaps it is a more urgent and difficult task to establish communion with our fellow humans. Listening to each other is the fundamental step.

Extending Constant Six into Daily Life

Listening from the heart is rooted in a deep desire to understand and be touched by the experience of another and to be of loving service by bearing witness to the story of a life. The value of applying this capacity in our family life, our work life, and our communities seems self-evident. As much as we want a world of peace, realistically we would settle for less conflict, less violence, less hostility, and less pain. The wisdom circle is a training arena for wakefulness and lovingkindness in all of our relationships, a place to experience the inner peace that must accompany any lasting peace in the world. Simply put, we enter into a state of profound resonance in which both listener and speaker dwell "in the center of things" and learn how to remain connected heart to heart.

SUMMARY OF CONSTANT SIX:

Listen from the heart, and serve as compassionate witness for the other people in the circle. To be an effective witness, pay attention to what is being said without interrupting, judging, or trying to "fix" or rescue the person speaking. Be willing to discover something about yourself in the stories of other people.

To listen a soul into disclosure and discovery is the greatest service one human being can do for another.

—Quaker saying

SEVEN

Speak from the Heart and from Direct Experience

The voice emerges from the body as a representation of our inner world. It carries our experience from the past, our hopes and fears for the future, and the emotional resonance of the moment.

—*David Whyte,* The Heart Aroused

This wisdom circle is a sacred place where we find our authentic voice—the one that contributes to the wisdom of the whole. Finding our own courage, strength, and wisdom, knowing that they are alive and well within each of us, will make it possible for others to find those qualities within themselves. May every person in this circle become the seed for a hundred new ideas and for ten creative solutions to each problem we face.

Amazing things happen when the wisdom circle becomes a safe place for people to speak from the heart. Shy people slowly overcome their reticence. People who are facile with words begin to find a voice that is more authentic. Sometimes tears of joy or sorrow well up when you recognize another person's story as your own. Initial nervousness gives way to relaxation when you dare to speak your heart and you feel heard. The excitement in the air is palpable when individual visions coalesce into a shared sense of purpose. Healing comes when you can laugh at yourself.

Wisdom Is an Emergent Quality of a Wisdom Circle

In the safety of a wisdom circle, people tell stories and reveal insights that inform and inspire and add to the storehouse of wisdom that all participants carry within themselves. As the saying goes, "It's in every one of us." The "it" refers to the elemental wisdom about what it means to be human, what it means to love one another, to do our best work, be our best selves. Sometimes that wisdom tells us to let go of beliefs that don't serve us anymore, how to bear the pain that comes into our lives, and when to get help rather than go it alone. We intuitively know how to do these things—humans have been doing them for thousands of years—but it sometimes takes a special setting, free of the noise of everyday life, to remember the wisdom, to draw it out of ourselves.

Wisdom, as we're using the word, is an "emergent quality" that can surface when individuals agree to enter into a small group with a loving heart and open mind for the purpose of mutual discovery. Bread emerges from yeast and flour and water. The *wisdom* of a wisdom circle consists of the words and emotions of direct experience woven together within a safe container. The "yeast" in a wisdom circle is truth-telling. Through storytelling, dream-telling, and plumbing the depths of our best and worst moments, we bring into the light our collected wisdom. It has the unmistakable quality of serving the whole.

Author Helen Luke tells us: "A real story touches not only the mind but also the imagination and the unconscious depths in a person, and it may remain with him or her for many years, coming to the surface of consciousness now and then to yield new insights." Stories are the currency of human learning and when told and retold to others, both speaker and story change, revealing the story's deeper meaning. Circle members work in partnership—speaker and listeners—to reveal the essence of each other's stories and call forth their illumination.

Finding Our Authentic Voice

Poet and writer David Whyte, in his book *The Heart Aroused*, observes:

> *The voice emerges literally from the body as a representation of our inner world. It carries our experience from the past, our hopes and fears for the future, and the emotional resonance of the moment. If it carries none of these it must be a masked voice, and having muted the voice, anyone listening knows intuitively we are not all there. Whether or not we try to tell the truth, the very act of speech is courageous because no matter what we say, we are revealed.*

Whyte goes on to say that in our first attempts at courageous speech we may wish to roar with the confidence of a lion and deliver, instead, the squeak of a mouse. Then, "if mouse is all we have, a first courageous step might be to say mouse is what we have to work with." It is better, Whyte points out, to have the timid squeak of a mouse than the arrogant roar of a lion that scares everyone to death. In other words, it is better to first develop the honesty and humility that accompany authenticity. People who come on with strong voices are sometimes masking the fears of their "inner mouse" and may be, in fact, less authentic and courageous than the more timid folks.

When you are moved to speak in a wisdom circle, select your words with care and thoughtfulness. Avoid abstract, conceptual language or a tutorial tone. Stay as closely in touch with your feelings as possible. In the beginning, most people have a tendency to be so engrossed in rehearsing what they're going to say when the talking stick reaches them that they miss much of what was said by others. In time, as we practice speaking from the heart, we learn not to rehearse our remarks; we learn that we don't need to prepare what we're going to say in advance of our turn to speak. Our comments are less premeditated and more spontaneous. We may even be surprised by what we say. Feelings are complex and can even be contradictory. But we begin to trust the words that are arising, the images pressing to be born. The following stories were triggered by the request to "Tell us a healing story":

During my internship as a surgeon I saw an older woman who'd been diagnosed with a large malignant tumor in her throat. My colleagues and I tried to con-

vince her that surgery was her only hope. She refused and said her faith in God would cure it. After trying several times to get her to change her mind, we gave up in frustration and wrote her off as being uneducated and misguided. Three months later she returned for a checkup. A first-year resident came to tell me there was no sign of cancer. I didn't believe him, checked her myself, and it was true. Maybe I was the one who was uneducated and misguided.

•

I was going to attend a three-day conference in the city where my father lived. We hadn't spoken to each other in over ten years. On a whim I decided to let him know I'd be in town and maybe we could get together. I left a message on his phone machine, not knowing how he'd respond. He called me back and said he'd like for me to stay with him while I was at the conference, paid for my plane ticket and asked me to stay a few extra days. I did, and we're in regular communication now. I can't tell you how happy I am that I made that call. The theme of the conference was "The Spirit of Healing."

At the end of someone's turn, you might want to register some feeling of attunement with the speaker, yet not take a full turn with the stick. It's perfectly fine to chime in with "May it be so" or "Amen" or "Right on." In Quaker circles, a familiar response is, "Thee has spoken after my own heart." The word "Ho" is used in some Native American circles and has the meaning of "I add my voice to yours."

~

Bringing Our Medicine to the Circle

In English the word "medicine," commonly used, means "that which heals." "Our own original medicine" is a phrase often heard in Native American circles. To "bring your medicine to the circle" means to bring what is uniquely yours and to be a full contributor to the beauty of the whole.

According to Native American teacher Jamie Sams, part of the work you do for your tribe is determining what your particular "medicine" is. Through praying, fasting, or going on a vision quest, you can make progress in discovering who you are, learning why you're here and what talents you possess to assist the whole tribe. Sams advises each of us: "Open up and allow others to see your Medicine. In that way, you are offering a gift to others who may have need of your talents. Every person carries a legacy of needed talents that will support the growth and expansion of a Tribe."

> *I remember a circle in which the main question was: "What sustains you during difficult times?" Story after story in that circle drew us closer together. We had a collective experience that allowed us to tap into a place of wisdom where everyone learned from each other. That circle was very magical.*

Our medicine may be a talent we are born with, something we learn over the course of our lives, or something we are compelled by circumstances to comprehend and express in the world. As we speak from the heart, we each offer a piece of our medicine to the others. Theologian

Henri Nouwen helps us understand how this process works:

> *It is remarkable how much consolation and hope we can receive from authors who, while offering no answers to life's questions, have the courage to articulate the situation of their lives in all honesty and directness. Kierkegaard, Sartre, Camus, Hammarskjöld and Merton—none of them—have ever offered solutions. Yet many of us who have read their works have found new strength to pursue our own search. Their courage to enter so deeply into human suffering and to become present to their own pain gave them the power to speak healing words.*

As we share our medicine, the life experiences we've distilled, it becomes part of the larger truth of the circle. How Gwen raises a disabled child, how Jeff lives with a life-threatening illness, how Nancy found the courage to go for a job that pays less and offers more spirit, how Dolores stood up to her boss when he suggested a sexual liaison, how Martin found ways to teach his science class about the value of the wilderness. Stories become part of the lore of the group, and, more than that, they become shared history. Other members are inspired to develop and express their own medicine. We all come to realize that life offers a variety of viewpoints and options in any challenge or situation we face.

~

What's Learnin' Ya?

Many wisdom circles have an issue or topic that participants have agreed will serve as their "center." But many others use the check-in approach to make topics surface for the meeting. Cultural anthropologist Angeles Arrien, who has studied many indigenous cultures, has given us an all-purpose question that usually elicits much "from the heart" material. It is simply, "What's learnin' ya?" or "What's workin' ya?" Her question turns our usual perception on its head. To ask "What challenges are you confronting today?" puts the emphasis on ego and control. By asking "What is learning you?" we are reminded that the experiences of life are our finest and harshest teachers.

What's learnin' me today is that my eighteen-year-old son was arrested again yesterday for possessing drugs. I just don't know what to do. I've bailed him out of jail. I've said I'll do anything to help him get clean. It's breaking my heart. I keep asking myself, and him, "what did we do wrong?" He says it's nothing we've done. He loves me; he says he loves his dad. He says he has to work this one out for himself. But it's so hard for me to let him do that.

•

I just don't know how to carry on my work in the organization anymore. It seems we've made so little progress against the companies that are polluting the bay. They keep doing it even when we win in the courts and they have to pay fines. We're like annoying gnats to them. Does anybody care that we can't eat fish from the bay anymore? Does anybody care that birds nesting in the marshes are having deformed chicks? I care. I care a lot. But I feel so despairing. How bad does it have to get before there's a real public outcry? Pretty bad, I guess. I think I need to go somewhere where there are clean beaches and no pollution. I've been so caught up in the ugliness. I need some beauty in my life.

Initially you may hold back your anger, your bitterness, or your sorrow about "what's workin' ya." You may be reluctant to reveal what you're anxious about. Or you may find yourself trying to put a positive spin on painful and private realities, trying to shut out what seems too hurtful or confusing to speak about. In time, members of the group develop trust and caring for each other, and things begin to change. Here is an example from Sedonia [Cahill]:

My women's lodge has been meeting for over fifteen years and we've talked about many topics, including aging and death, our own deaths. We spent several meetings telling our sexual history from beginning to end. With that topic we were all able to laugh and cry together as we discovered that the telling of these stories wasn't hard to do. Then we decided to talk about money. In the first evening it was amazing to find that this group of very competent women had so much shame and embarrassment talking about it. We had no difficulty in our meetings about sex, or death. But money was hard to talk about.

There were tears as we told stories revealing how mystifying money was to each of us. Somehow we hadn't been raised to understand it. We had mismanaged our own money, lost money, and almost never asked for the amount of money we deserved for our work. There was guilt about having money, guilt about not having money. For middle-class women of our generation, talking about money had been a family taboo. We stayed with this subject for several meetings because it was so potent, and each time I dreaded going to the circle, thinking, "I really don't want to face this." After that, each woman in the group took various steps to get a handle on the issue. I know I did. Those circles changed our lives.

•

I was very upset with my husband. I'd been expressing my anger for several meetings. One of the women said very quietly to me, "Where's the heart? Where's the love in your relationship?" I didn't have an answer. This shocked me. I took that question home, and I knew I had to change something. That was a very simple and subtle thing she said to me, but it was huge in terms of making me look differently at my relationship.

When you speak your pain or concern aloud in the presence of others, you may find the courage to work through it. You feel it rather than suppress it and then, at a time that feels right to you, you can express it. You allow it to inform you, and hopefully you learn from it. It comes to light rather than lurking in the shadows.

Gradually, there is a greater and greater congruence between who you *are* and who you believe yourself to be, and how you represent yourself to others. Instead of competing with one another for attention and trying to prove that we are special, we come to accept one another—and ourselves—as we are. A community can develop as we share a common openness and vulnerability. We become willing to remove the barriers that prevent us from entering into communion with others in the circle. We seek what social activist Fran Peavey calls "the strength not to be greater or lesser than my brother or sister but to remove the tough and slimy obstacles to equality that have made their home inside myself."

Dojo: A Place to Practice a Way of Being in the World

An analogy exists between a wisdom circle and a martial arts training room, called a *dojo*. What you learn in a *dojo* regarding balance, assertiveness, and flexibility is meant to be taken into your daily life. So, too, in a wisdom circle, the practice of speaking from the heart is meant to become second nature to you. The circle is also a place to improve our ability to give voice to and communicate our essential truths.

In a practice arena of any kind, you are encouraged to stretch yourself. This is the place to be a beginner, make mistakes. This is the place you can allow yourself to look foolish, ignorant, or neurotic. In one wisdom circle, Rebecca never fails to update the group on how her mother is doing and the state of their relationship. Group members have taken to gently kidding her about her unusual attachment to her mom. Yet it feels to them that Rebecca's mom has almost become part of the group. What could have been a possible source of irritation has become part of Rebecca's medicine to the group. Her mom's well-being and their relationship have become part of the group's tapestry.

Every circle has norms and limits. Over time it will be clear what's in bounds and what's out of bounds in terms of content and focus for the group. As they build trust and solidarity among members, many groups then move on to consider "tough" questions and to explore personal feelings and experiences having to do with racism, sexism, homophobia, religion, and other potentially divisive subjects. If certain group members want to explore a difficult topic, it is best to check with each member to see if such a focus is okay with everyone. Speaking from the heart on racism may mean someone reveals the racist stereotypes she was raised with. Speaking from the heart on homosexuality may mean someone says he feels strongly that such behavior is a "sin." The feelings of members who might be spoken about in unkind or insensitive ways must be taken into account. On the other hand, overt sexist, racist, or homophobic behavior of one member toward another should be addressed when it happens. (For more help on this, see Chapter 15.)

It is important to remember that we have no right to tell truths about ourselves at the expense of someone else. You may want to talk about an affair you're having that's hurting your family, but your family may not want that information revealed. Your truth-telling should not involve invading the privacy of another group member.

We advise that if there is one person in the group who objects to a topic or fears being hurt, or hurting someone else, the topic be shelved for the time being. A commitment to meeting regularly in a discipline of honest searching will provide a basis for greater trust. More practice in speaking from the heart may eventually allow for challenging topics to be addressed. As group members come to know each other better, someone may want to suggest the topic again.

Just as in a *dojo* you know the dangers of attempting some move beyond your skill level, so too in a wisdom circle you must exercise common sense about what the skills of the group are at any given time. It takes an honest level of trust, cohesion, and a time of "building up to" in order to tackle difficult topics.

Becoming Better Storytellers

When we speak from the heart, the idea is not to hook the listener or offer a compelling ending to the story but to communicate the reasons it was told. We tell a story first and foremost to extract its wisdom for ourselves and then feel blessed when it offers wisdom to others as well. In her book *Kitchen Table Wisdom*, Rachel Naomi Remen says that sharing our stories requires that we stop, reflect, and wonder, and make our journey conscious:

> *Until we stop ourselves, or more often, have been stopped, we hope to put certain of life's events "behind us" and get on with our living. After we stop we see that certain of life's issues will be with us for as long as we live. We will pass through them again and again, each time with a new story, each time with a greater understanding, until they become indistinguishable from our blessings and our wisdom. It's the way life teaches us how to live.*

~

Dr. Remen has heard many stories in her years as a physician and medical director of the Commonweal Cancer Help

Program in Bolinas, California. Her experience has gained her the insight that on a soul level all stories are equal: "Everyone's story matters. The wisdom in the story of the most educated and powerful person is often not greater than the wisdom in the story of a child, and the life of a child can teach us as much as the life of a sage."

Our stories resonate with the unconscious levels of our personality and work deeply within us as a powerful structuring force. As we increase our capacity to speak from the heart, we may continue to pick up these unconscious aspects of our lives and begin to hear a deeper story we are trying to tell.

> *As I told the story of my three days of solo time during the vision quest to the rest of the questers, I thought I would have to say that I really didn't have a vision or any great insight during that time. I had gone to the desert seeking a more "embedded" relationship with nature. Then I remembered an incident during the second day when rain clouds were threatening. I was sincerely hoping it wouldn't rain and cause me to have to deal with wet clothes and mud. I took refuge under my tarp and about a dozen drops of rain fell. Then nothing for forty-five minutes. I peeked out and the clouds had passed. Relieved, I came out of my shelter. I was grateful that it hadn't rained. Then all at once I looked around and was struck by how dry and thirsty everything looked—all the scrub pine trees and sagebrush. They would have loved for it to rain. I had only seen how it would have inconvenienced me. In that moment I received a lesson in "considering the whole" whenever I ask for some-*

thing. Telling that story allowed the lesson to become a permanent part of my awareness.

We stand at the center of our stories. It is how we emerge from them and how we are changed by telling them that is important, not simply how the story ends. Ideally, the speaker and the listeners will begin to sense the living core of the narrative and tune into the deeper message. Not every story has a happy or even an insightful ending, but each of us is invited into the circle to share our medicine—to gift to others the benefit of our hard-earned experience—not merely those parts that are uplifting, inspiring, and easy to share with others.

Inviting the Shadow In

Psychologists speak of our "shadow side" or "shadow elements" in our unconscious, which are aspects of ourselves that we repress from our conscious awareness. They include negative personality characteristics, wounding experiences, patterns that we keep repeating and don't want to see. The Swiss psychiatrist Carl Jung believed the shadow also included the positive elements about ourselves, such as latent talents, that we have yet to acknowledge—the light we hide under the bushel basket. Members in a safe, caring circle know they can invite the shadow aspects of their story and themselves to make an appearance.

We had known Margaret through the circle for over a year when she asked some of us to read an essay she had written. It contained a shocking story about how she had been molested by her father when she was a teenager. In it she also talked about her anger toward her mother for allowing the violation to go on. Margaret said she couldn't have told the story in the circle, but having us read it opened the door for her to talk about the effects this had had on her life.

•

A circle member was grossly overweight, had labored breathing, and was looking quite unhealthy. She had never brought up any mention of her weight in the circle. When someone else decided to finally bring up the issue of her health, she spoke for perhaps the first time about how she felt her eating habits were out of her control. Some people in the circle who felt close to her offered to help. She is now reaching out to them for support as she continues to lose weight.

•

Another circle decided to watch the film The Color of Fear, *which documents a powerful exchange on the issue of racism in America among nine men representing four races. In recounting their experience of watching the film, some of the circle members were reluctant to give voice to the racial stereotypes they were raised with. No one expected that one evening would undo decades of social conditioning, but the circle felt that the courage its members exhibited in introducing the topic in a direct and powerful way spoke volumes about the kind of community they were forming.*

Direct Experience

Speaking from direct experience is essential because it is our most trustworthy source. We learn in circle that our experience is our highest authority. As we listen deeply to our stories, we discover that we don't need experts to guide our journey as much as a clear inner attunement. When speaking from direct experience, we learn, often to our surprise, that what is most personal is most universal. We come to realize that it is precisely our most personal and private thoughts and feelings that speak most deeply to others when shared in circle.

In a wisdom circle there is no need to defend a set of beliefs. We care more about deep truth-telling than asserting ourselves, competing with others, or achieving dominance. There's no one "right way" to feel. Does that mean that a wisdom circle cannot accommodate abstract or strategic discussions? It's possible that a circle will want to address a topic that invites conceptual discussion or theorizing. Public mental-health workers may want to discuss ways to improve service to the community. A *Celestine Prophecy* study group may wish to explore how that book's insights apply to their personal lives. A caregiving organization may want to discuss how to reduce the hierarchical structure of the agency. Or a group of eco-activists may want to plan a demonstration to halt the clear-cutting of an old-growth forest.

We have found that when a theoretical or strategic discussion is needed, holding a wisdom circle prior to or after the discussion is helpful. The circle format lends itself well to drawing out and on the experiences of group members. It also serves to temper the quality of the discussion so that participants are more open to hearing each other. Remember that a wisdom circle can be combined with other formats such as a standard meeting, a lecture, or out-of-circle dialogue as long as the Ten Constants are adhered to during the wisdom circle. The beginning and end of the circle itself will be marked by the opening and closing rituals.

SUMMARY OF CONSTANT SEVEN:

Speak from the heart and from direct experience. When you are moved to speak, do so thoughtfully and with care. Avoid abstract, conceptual language, and stay in touch with your feelings as deeply as possible. As this capacity develops, you may be moved to share those feelings and to say difficult things without self-judgment and without blaming others.

EIGHT

Make Room for Silence to Enter

A silence that is like a lake, a smooth and compact surface. Down below, submerged, the words are waiting. And one must descend, go to the bottom, be silent, wait.

—*Octavio Paz,*
The Bow and the Lyre

Let's make room for silence to enter our wisdom circle. As we sit in silence together, we can better feel our soul connections. This is the time to clear our minds again, as we did in the opening ritual. This is the time for whatever has been hanging back in the recesses of our consciousness to show up and be heard.

(Please take some time, before you continue reading this chapter, to experience a deep silence, for however long you're comfortable. Then go on.)

The first time your wisdom circle sits in silence for longer than thirty seconds, there's bound to be some uneasiness. Who will fill the void? At least several people are thinking to themselves, "Will someone please pick up the stick and talk?" Two minutes of silence go by. After five minutes there are noticeable signs of discomfort. Someone will pick up the stick, not moved to speak from his or her experience, but simply to release the building tension.

Getting acquainted with the power of silence takes practice. People in the group who happen to be experienced meditators might choose to go into a meditative state, but others may be struggling with the sense of "empty time" and "nothing's happening." To be in silence in this way requires the ability to surrender to the wordless place within. Eventually, sitting in silence will produce a new kind of attunement. Naturally, it will take time before harmony is achieved and everyone feels in synch.

Creating the Space for Something Deeper to Show Up

The most important thing to understand about the eighth constant is that a period of silence does not mean that "nothing is happening." It is not just some sort of hiatus or respite from the important activities of the group. Silence provides the essential atmosphere for you to access the hidden places in your psyche, the places where important memories are stored and deep feelings reside—including the ones that make you feel vulnerable to the judgment of others. Silence may allow the more intuitive responses to surface and leave space for new images to suggest themselves.

For the person holding the talking object, silence offers permission to sense whether you have finished speaking, or if there is an even deeper message in the experience you are sharing. Listeners can clear their minds and cultivate a state of receptivity and openness. To use Octavio Paz's phrase, the silence helps calm the lake, creating the smooth surface so the speaker can feel secure in descending toward the bottom. Each person's intuitive voice can be better heard when this calm descends upon the circle.

Silence allows the soul its preferred context, that of receptivity and contemplation—a stillness that beckons the authentic self to emerge. Eugene Gendlin, author of *Focusing*, says silence often helps us move beyond self-limiting concepts: "At first the words and feeling may be exactly all one, but after a while [of sitting in silence], you will find the feeling growing somewhat longer, sticking out around the edges of the words." In silence, the mind has permission to move beyond words and to experience the depth of our feelings. This is the entranceway to what the mystics call the realm of "sensation without thought" where we discover the essential self.

Normally we experience our thoughts coming from a process we call "thinking." Even when there are heavy emotional overtones to those thoughts, they still have the quality of being formed by a rational process. When you have the experience of words coming from a deeper place within, from your heart, or your gut, they have a different quality. The words are, most often, simpler, not hedged with qualifications, excuses, or face-saving phrases. From this place we do not make disclaimers such as, "It didn't matter to me, but . . ." or, "I'm not sure what you'll think of me if I say this but . . ." or, "This probably sounds stupid but. . . ." Instead, the speaker tends to use simple, straightforward language: "I think . . ."; "I feel . . ."; "It's my experience that . . ."

Allowing silence to enter encourages us to speak from the heart. It also helps us develop a sensitivity to subtle cues and timing. A circle has its own rhythm, and the intuitive feel we develop for the group helps us to decide when to speak and when not to. Sometimes we are more nourished by the silence than by our words. In time we realize how nourished we are by the *whole* process—by the words and by the silence—that unfolds in a wisdom circle.

Silence Is an Endangered Species

Most of us live in a world where noise is the norm. Some people must have the sounds of a TV, a radio, music, a computer, or the hum of some appliance, going on all the time. Silence makes them nervous. Massive noise pollution has invaded human life in the past one hundred years that now seems like water to a fish—noise has become our "natural" environment. Learning to make friends with silence may be akin to withdrawal from an addictive drug—one that dulls the senses and deprives us of a pristine quality in our own experiences.

Establishing an external silence may be difficult enough, but the kind of silence that most benefits a wisdom circle is our inner one. Theologian Henri Nouwen observes:

> *When all the daily racket is shut off, a new noise turns on, rising out of all those vague feelings which scream for attention. . . . The many unsolved problems demand attention, one care forces itself upon another, one complaint rivals the next, all plead for hearing.*

Nouwen points out that one of the reasons we cling to external noise is to shut out all those voices within ourselves. Learning how to sit calmly and quietly, then sort through the voices vying for attention in our mind, is one of the capacities that gets developed within the wisdom circle.

Learning How to Swim in Emptiness

Learning how to make room for silence is a little like learning how to swim. Remember the first time you were in water over your head? You had to focus on staying calm and moving your arms and legs in a coordinated fashion. The more you developed an economy in your effort, the better you swam. A kind of disciplined learning process characterizes both swimming and maintaining silence. When we learn to focus and stay centered, we can move beyond the automatic judgments and unexamined assumptions that clutter up our minds. With an economy of effort, we find a place of profound stillness and receptivity within. Attending to ourselves in the grace of that stillness, we discover the ground of our own wisdom. Silence reveals; silence heals; silence helps us locate ourselves.

Like the space between musical notes or the white of a Chinese watercolor, the "emptiness" is as important as the other major elements. We need to know how to empty ourselves so that new thoughts, feelings, and images may rise from the unconscious. Becoming comfortable in the company of others in silence is one of the challenges, and gifts, of a wisdom circle.

As you grow to appreciate the role of silence in a wisdom circle, you'll experience how it enhances *temenos*, the feeling of being in sacred time and space. When we enter into a cathedral, a temple, an ashram, a zendo, we lower our voices, we speak less. This is also true for those moments when we behold the special grace of nature—entering a grove of trees, exploring a cave, or walking along the ocean. Sacred space and silence go hand in hand. They both expand our capacity for listening and speaking from the heart.

Comfortably being silent together in a group has a way of bonding the participants. Collective silence modulates the pace of a circle and motivates a contemplative attitude; it encourages the reticent to speak; it lessens the feeling of competition with the more glib or verbose people in the group. Shy people feel the quiet time allows them to collect their thoughts, and anxious people find it allows them to center themselves.

> *We've found it useful in our circle to be mindful of the gifts of silence and encourage it to enter. When it feels appropriate, someone suggests that we all chant the Sanskrit syllable "om" together and then let the sound just die away. Then we sit and appreciate the qualities silence has. When someone is moved to speak, we continue.*

Extending Silence into Our Daily Lives

Taking the time to let periods of silence enter your life might appear to be a luxury you can't afford. But mystics, writers, poets, and artists of all kinds have said that sitting in silence is the only way inspiration and connection with the sacred come to them. Appreciating the richness of silence in a wisdom circle may hopefully encourage you to find similar moments in daily life.

For more inspiration, we will turn again to Gunilla Norris, from her book *Sharing Silence*: "By making room for silence, we resist the forces of the world which tell us to live an advertised life of surface appearances, instead of a discovered life—a life lived in contact with our senses, our feelings, our deepest thoughts and values."

SUMMARY OF CONSTANT EIGHT:

**Make room
for silence to enter.
During the circle, allow
for reflection, meditation,
for deep feelings to sur-
face. Silence enhances
temenos as the group
proceeds.**

NINE

Empower Each Member to Be a Co-facilitator of the Process

Guidance is internal.

—Words spoken in the countdown for the Apollo Eleven moon launch fifteen seconds before takeoff

Let us be companions in the quest that never ceases—the inquiry into who we are and why we are here. We remind each other of our inner truths and support each other in living our beauty. What a rare experience! to feel equally empowered to hold the circle, to question the process, to be held as vital and sacred by the others.

Two of the most important questions asked by circle members are "How is leadership designated in a wisdom circle?" and "What model of leadership and group facilitation do we use?" We suggest a model of stewardship whereby each member functions as a full partner and takes equal responsibility for group process. This is the ideal. What really happens in your wisdom circle will depend on many factors, including members' experience with circle work, the level of cohesiveness, or shared focus, in the group, and the individual personalities of the participants. Not everyone will feel comfortable taking a turn at being the circle maker, and no one should ever be forced to. However, as others offer to co-lead and provide support, some reluctant members may be persuaded that the wisdom circle is strengthened by everyone's participation—by each person's way of opening it and giving focus to the content.

The Role of Wisdom Circle Maker

We suggest that each meeting have a designated circle maker who is responsible for setting up the physical environment, including the chairs and central table or cloth, and for devising the opening and closing rituals. Ideally, this role should rotate so that every member gets the opportunity to create the environment in which the circle is begun. Usually one person takes the initiative to begin a circle, anyway. Chances are, she or he has a colleague, friend, or coworker who is equally enthusiastic. They may take on the circle-maker role the first few meetings and then alternate with someone else who is willing to do it. Gradually, as more and more members assume the role, we see that each person in the circle brings a unique way of adding color and order to the circle process, one that benefits the entire group. The group may also decide to divide the duties of the circle maker. Having only one responsibility at a meeting, such as leading the opening ritual or suggesting the central question, may encourage more people to volunteer.

In Part 2 of the book, we will go into more detail on the calling of the circle, opening and closing rituals, and starter questions. We encourage you to be as creative as you can with these aspects of circle making.

It may turn out that someone never takes on the role of circle maker, even when it is made as unimposing as possible. As with any group, members play a variety of important roles. Group dynamics expert Arnold Mindell says that each and every role in a group is important to what he calls the group's "field."

> *Even if your role is to be the silent one who feels but cannot speak, you are essential to the field. You may play an unpopular or even a publicly unrecognized role but you still play a "leading" role in the sense that only when all roles are consciously represented, can the field operate humanely and wisely. Each role is a leading one because the field we live in is created by the tension and interaction between all its roles.*

Mindell's "field" idea is similar to field theory in physics, which describes the dynamic interaction among particles. The "aliveness" of a wisdom circle comes from the synergy and the diversity of its participants. Roles will shift as people find the courage to express various parts of their personalities. We might fill alternately the roles of circle maker, leader, follower, silent one, wise one, clown, conscience, disrupter, needy one, and so on, as we take part in an ongoing wisdom circle. It is best to let someone pass on the circle maker role if it really doesn't fit until such time that it does. The intention of the ninth constant is to encourage a sense of self-empowerment and equal responsibility for the well-being and functioning of the group.

The Necessity of Speaking Up

The designated circle maker has explicit tasks to carry out, but during the activities of listening and speaking, he or she is an equal member of the group. It's very important that each member be aware of his or her responsibilities to the circle and seek proactively to fulfill them. These responsibilities include the following:

1. **Maintain a safe space for everyone in the circle.**
2. **Involve as many members as possible in determining the group focus.**
3. **Encourage all members to participate through deep truth-telling.**
4. **Help the circle to stay on track, and, when necessary, remind members of its original purpose.**
5. **Acknowledge feelings of tension or conflict.**
6. **Acknowledge the bond between members and what the circle contributes to your life.**
7. **Make explicit any expectations you have for the circle.**
8. **Be aware of the Ten Constants, and bring them to the group's attention when any are being neglected.**

When things are going smoothly, the circle is essentially directing itself. Each person serves as a positive role model for other members and as a steward of the circle without falling into a consistent leader or follower role. Members resist the inclination to dominate the circle and thereby deprive other members of the opportunity to express their truths. They also resist passivity and the tendency to let the circle be dominated by the most verbal members. Everyone must monitor their tendencies toward dependent and/or controlling behaviors and invite their fellow circle members to point it out when they feel such behavior is holding back the full potential of the circle. Each member thereby brings his or her unique leadership capacities to the group.

Initially, we may feel strange or embarrassed to make comments about the way things are going in circle, but if we are feeling that something is amiss, chances are good someone else also feels the need for a change in course. The following comments illustrate efforts at co-facilitation on the part of circle members:

It's fine for us to disagree in circle and express our anger and frustration, but we've also agreed to respect one another's rights to express a different point of view.

•

It seems that Tom, Sally, and Hector have been doing most of the talking this evening, and the rest of us have been saying very little.

•

I know I'm interrupting an important topic, but it looks like several of us have disengaged from the round and seem irritated or bored right now. Am I right?

•

I'm feeling very uncomfortable right now, and I need to check this out. Does anybody else feel the same?

When even one member who has been withdrawn feels empowered to state an uncomfortable feeling about the circle process, the entire circle is empowered. When members comment on cross-talk or the apparent disinterest of fellow participants, they give others permission to comment in a similar fashion. When anyone observes that a usually talkative member seems very sad or that a member's question to the group has been ignored, he or she models co-facilitation for the other members.

Guidance Is Internal

There resides in each one of us, we believe, a desire to be our own authority, trust our own judgments, and speak our truth. A wisdom circle provides a way of giving life to that desire. Establishing the authority of your own voice is also necessary for the overall strength of the circle. If you've ever heard the famous countdown of the Apollo Eleven mission that took Neil Armstrong, Buzz Aldrin, and Mike Collins to the moon, you heard the voice of Houston Control say, "19, 18, 17, 16, guidance is internal, 13, 12. . . ." At takeoff minus fifteen seconds the primary controls switched from Ground Control to the rocket itself. When psychologists describe the maturation process, they say we shift from a more external locus of control to a more internal one. As we develop into healthy adults, we assume a greater sense of authority for our actions. We move from a primary dependence on outside authorities such as parents, teachers, clergy, older siblings, and so forth, to a more internally determined sense of order. How successfully we negotiate that shift toward self-authorization is a primary index of our mental and emotional well-being—and of how much we can assume responsibility for our own lives.

Most of us don't think about our sources of guidance as we make daily evaluations and decisions. So much of what we consider our own thinking is actually a blend of ideas handed down to us by our parents, our subculture, our religion, and those sources we've chosen as credible. We don't stop to question how we arrived at the ideas that help us interpret what goes on around us. If we took the time to analyze our personal guidance system, we would probably discover that it is a hodgepodge of sources, conflicting values, and a lot of fuzziness and gray areas. How much of our behavior is the result of conscious intention and how much is unconsciously motivated? Even when we are most clear about our intentions, our behavior is strongly influenced by unconscious motives.

One of the ways that a wisdom circle can serve you is to provide a forum to examine your collection of beliefs and assumptions and arrive at a more cohesive, more conscious guidance system. Put simply, it is a practice arena for each of us to develop our internal guidance and be less beholden to those institutions or authorities who would prefer that we not question the political and socioeconomic systems now in place. As Buddhist scholar Joanna Macy says:

> *To discover what we know and we feel is not as easy as it sounds, because a great deal of effort in contemporary society is devoted to keeping us from being honest. Entire industries are focused on maintaining the illu-*

> *sion that we are happy, or on the verge of being happy as soon as we buy this toothpaste or that deodorant or that political candidate. It is not in the self-perceived interests of the state, the multinational corporations, or the media that serve them both, that we should stop and become aware of our profound anguish with the way things are.*
>
> *. . . The first discovery, opening to what we know and feel, takes courage. Like Gandhi's* satyagraha, *it involves "truth-force." People are not going to find their truth-force or inner authority in listening to the experts, but in listening to themselves, for everyone in her or his way is an expert on what it is like to live on an endangered planet.*

In short, the path to wisdom and growth goes through deep truth-telling.

To say, "My guidance is internal," does not mean that you somehow arrived at all your beliefs and your moral code all by yourself, with no input from others. It simply means that you are more aware of the ideas that inform your choices. For example, you might hold the deep-ecology view that all living beings are interdependent, or you might believe that the world is a hierarchy with humans at the top. And what set of assumptions do you have about the nature of reality? You might only credit what you can perceive with the senses, or you might believe in a metaphysical or spiritual reality with unmapped dimensions. To truly say, "My guidance is internal," means you are aware of the views and moral code you have adopted and have a sense of how and why they work for you. Not many of us can claim to operate from such a consistent base of beliefs. But we can keep working at it.

People often think the amount of control they exert in their lives is a measure of self-authorization. Realistically, of course, we're beholden to an appreciable extent to outside authorities for our legal and societal norms. We may also choose to give over our sense of inner authority to a "higher power" in the form of a religion or a spiritual path. Many of us also choose to submit to the authority of, and adopt the perspective of, the military service, a political party, a corporation, or maybe even a domineering life partner. How much of the day do you feel that you are speaking and acting based on your own consciously chosen set of ethics, your own closely held values, and your own intuition? It is probably safe to assume the answer is, "Not enough of the time."

Your internal guidance is also vital in monitoring your comfort level with the group. One way is to check out how your body is feeling. Because our emotions register as changes in our bodies, pay attention to tightness in your throat or an unsettled feeling in your stomach. Give voice to whatever change or discomfort you feel and to your best interpretation of the cause. A member might ask the group to stop for a minute, close their eyes, and take turns saying what physical sensations they're having at that moment. The cornerstone value of the wisdom circle is that each member is the ultimate authority of his or her experience and feelings. Our most trustworthy source of guidance is internal.

Co-evolution: The Circle and Its Members

Every circle has its own developmental process and its own way of achieving depth and cohesion. In time, every member can develop as a steward and as a proactive partner. We, the authors, have learned through participating in many circles that the constants play an important role in increasing everyone's sense of empowerment. "I've found that the more I commit and contribute to the circle, the more the circle becomes stronger and healthier," says Mike, who's been in men's and mixed gender circles for over ten years. "And it's real clear to me that the stronger the circle is, the more I benefit." It is a paradox of the circle that the more we are bonded as a group, the more important our contributions as individuals become.

One of the commitments we explicitly make within a wisdom circle is to embrace diversity among people, not only because it is humane to do so but because it is key to our survival. We will simply not survive as a species if we continue to judge, discriminate against, torture, and kill each other because of differences in race, religion, gender, ideology, or sexual orientation. We know in our hearts that although we may say we are committed to equality in our society, our rhetoric does not match the reality that people of color or those who are aged, disabled, poor, or obese, experience every day. Some of us also consciously or unconsciously accord more status to people who are more educated, more articulate, more affluent, or more charismatic than others.

In a wisdom circle we can begin to unlearn the conditioned

stereotypes that live in us, which often become obstacles to our directly experiencing other human beings and to recognizing the fundamental equality between us. Our relationships in a wisdom circle are forged in a group process that explicitly values full and free communication, recognizes cultural and social differences as strengths, and has as one of its goals the flowering of each person to their full potential.

One woman found herself feeling fearful and suspicious about the nature of the circle she had joined at a women's recovery center. She felt as though it might violate her own religious beliefs. So she asked everyone if they would stand up and sing gospel songs with her. The group readily agreed and sang with joy and enthusiasm, some people better than others. This event brought everyone, including the woman who had made the request, into a closer and more bonded circle.

•

Two employees of a small business were having interpersonal problems, so the owner decided to hold a wisdom circle to air everyone's feelings. The circle maker began by asking each person to say what he or she liked about working there. Then she asked everyone to speak to the problems they were having. Jack, who worked part-time in the shipping department, was also an intern from a drug-recovery halfway house. He remained silent throughout most of the circle. As the talking object passed for the final round, the question was: "What commitment can you make toward improving the quality of communication around here?" Jack began by saying, "I've never been involved in something like this, where everybody was so honest about their feelings.

Hearing all of you talk has made me see the value of it. You can count me in as someone who'll be more upfront about my feelings. But most of all, you can count on me to listen to each of you with an open mind and keep you honest too."

Constant Nine has the effect of leveling certain differences such as age and educational background because it holds that each person is there to share equally in the circle's responsibilities and benefits. The intention of Constant Nine is not only to share the activities of a circle in a functionally equal way but that each of us become aware of, and unlearn, the stereotypes that reinforce notions of superiority. Anything that even subtly suggests to a circle member that he or she is viewed as less than a full partner in the process *disempowers* that person. It undermines that person's sense of worth and denies that person safety to express his or her truths.

People come together carrying their baggage of biases and prejudices. Yet, in a wisdom circle, it is an ongoing task for members to develop a deep and abiding mutual respect among themselves. Circles may even ask a member to leave if repeated attempts at consciousness-raising fail, and she or he continues to speak or act in a way inconsistent with the intention of the ninth constant. Working to embrace the equality of each member is certainly "good practice," and helps build the more inclusive community we envision for the future.

Keeping the Constants Alive

The most important way that each member functions as a steward and co-creator of the circle is by remembering and reinforcing the Ten Constants. As the group's values and guidelines, they shape the wisdom circle process and have a marked impact on the way individuals participate in circle and think about themselves in relation to the group. The gradual incorporation of the constants promotes the sharing of power and responsibility. In time, we all become co-facilitators, and the constants become habits, traditions, and norms.

A wisdom circle that is a success in the estimation of all its members is not a "blessed accident." The circle succeeds because the members consciously and intuitively understand the dynamics of circle making. The Ten Constants help satisfy our individual needs for self-discovery and affiliation as well as the group's need to accomplish its mission of building compassionate community. The wisdom circle format enhances our capacity to learn and to grow in intimacy and to integrate the needs of each individual with the needs of the collective. You learn to trust the process; the circle itself becomes a teacher.

SUMMARY OF CONSTANT NINE:

Empower each member to be a co-facilitator of the process. If possible, designate a different person to be the circle maker each time. This person readies the physical setting, initiates the opening and closing rituals, and facilitates consensus on a topic. Encourage each other to give voice to feelings of satisfaction or discomfort about the group's process.

TEN

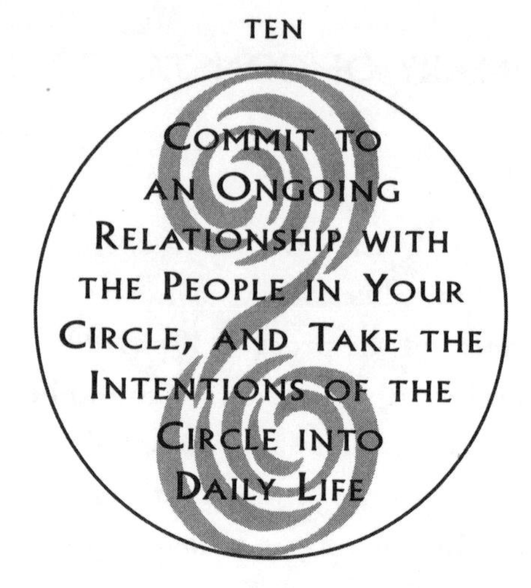

Commit to an Ongoing Relationship with the People in Your Circle, and Take the Intentions of the Circle into Daily Life

We need smaller groups now. . . . Hope a new class of people will know what's necessary. . . . It's these small groups of people who will lead in the eventual help . . . people who will be able to make the change to a higher place . . . their small risks will become law.

—Lewis Mumford during his dying time,
Lapis *magazine, No. 3*

I call upon you to witness my commitment to the circle, and to my own personal development. Within this community are gifts for healing the world, for learning to live in harmony with one another and with the Earth. The more I commit to the highest values held by this group, the more I am empowered to give voice to those values. I am present here to discover my own wisdom and compassion and to bear witness to yours. I am present for you. Thank you for being present for me.

In an ongoing circle, members need to assess their level of personal commitment by asking themselves certain questions. Will I attend every meeting unless something unavoidable happens to interfere? Will I be on time and stay for the full meeting? Will I honor the guidelines of the circle? Am I committed to self-exploration and to being present for the explorations of others? Will I speak my truth in the circle, even when it is hard and uncomfortable? Am I committed to staying alert and present and to bringing my mind, heart, and soul to the group? And finally, will I extend the intentions of the circle into my daily life?

If a circle is to fulfill its potential, these kinds of commitments are necessary. We need to be willing to show up. People come to know us only when we have met in circle many times together. We need to bear witness when any one of us is going through something difficult. When that kind of commitment is consistent, a wisdom circle becomes a *dojo*—a place where we can safely practice the ways we want to engage the world. The benefits of this work for group members can be immeasurable. Those outside the group may experience a ripple effect. What we do together radiates out from this center and gladdens the whole.

The Bedrock of Trust

Commitment and trust go hand in hand. In order to trust others with the most tender and vulnerable parts of ourselves, we need to feel that they will hold everything we say in the strictest confidence. We need to know that they won't turn away when we have exposed the darker, shadow sides of ourselves. That they won't withdraw or drop out when we most need their love and compassionate witnessing. That they won't run if we say something that challenges their beliefs or peace of mind. A wisdom circle expands its capacity to support and transform its members to the extent that it sows this trust.

After meeting monthly in a wisdom circle for well over a year, everyone felt they knew each other fairly well. It was a surprise when Molly had something to say that she felt might cause us to change our attitude toward her. She told us she was a closet alcoholic. She drank alone and at night, and she drank a lot. She asked the group to hold her to the commitment to end her drinking from that day forward. Molly kept her commitment. The group did too.

•

Nine people met weekly in a wisdom circle while watching each segment of a seven-part PBS series titled Reaching Out, *which dealt with community service and its role in ending racism and the assault on the environment. During a round of reflections, Althea, an African American woman, said she was angry about the recent stories on the CIA's involvement in the crack-cocaine epidemic in the inner cities. Cheryl, who's white, picked up the stick and held it in silence for a while. She said she too had been upset by this story, but living in an all-white suburb had blunted its impact on her. Cheryl said that hearing Althea speak of how the story affected her personally gave Cheryl a chance to feel the story "from the inside out."*

•

A dozen AIDS caregivers met for a day-long wisdom circle. At one point in the afternoon, they each told of an especially memorable exchange with a friend or client. Tears came to our eyes as we listened to stories of caring for the ravaged personalities and withering bodies of people dying with the disease. Almost everyone had spoken, and the stick was sitting in the middle. John slowly picked it up and said hesitantly: "The story I want to tell isn't like yours. A moment of truth came to me when I realized I could no longer cope with taking care of my lover of two years in his dying time. I felt overwhelmed with sadness, fear, guilt, just everything for wanting to quit. That was five years ago, and I'm still carrying the guilt of not having been there full-time." The group stayed silent as John wept, each of us realizing that his guilt could easily have been ours.

The trust level in each of these circles was enough to provide the safety for Molly and Cheryl and John to take a risk—to expose a vulnerable part of themselves without fear of censure or advice from the group. John mentioned later, in an out-of-circle dialogue, that he would never have been able to tell his story had he felt someone was going to try to "process" his feelings with him, as can happen in a traditional support group. It was because he knew that everyone was simply there to witness his truth, and not comment on it, that he had the courage to tell it. John could have asked for comments, but he didn't want to. Molly didn't want any advice either, only the commitment to witness her choice to stop drinking. Again, comments and advice are only offered when they are explicitly solicited by the speaker.

In all three instances, the commitment was to hear the individual out—to trust in the speaker's own ability to seek a resolution. But what happens when you ask for feedback and want to know whether others have any experience on the subject? You can put the talking stick in the middle and open the space to anyone, or you may hold the stick and acknowledge each person who wants to speak and thus control the flow of feedback by saying when you've heard enough.

Debbie asked her women's circle to hear her story and keep it in confidence. She and her husband were talking about separating. Several other women spoke about when they had been in similar circumstances. At the next meeting Debbie could barely wait for the check-in. During the interim, a woman in the group had phoned her husband and had flirtatiously asked him to meet her for lunch. Debbie was shocked, angry, and hurt. She asked the other women what their response would be. Each of them was able to speak from the heart and share her anger. They also spoke their feelings to the other woman, who admitted what she had done and said how sorry she was for her behavior and for violating the confidence of the group.

None of the members would have ever thought such a blatant violation of trust could occur in their wisdom circle. Breaches of trust and confidentiality do happen—as in the rest of life. A group can suffer an emotional wounding just as an individual does, and then it takes a period of time and effort for healing to take place.

Other kinds of expectations that may be confounding to the group can crop up too. What if a couple who are both members in the group decide to separate but both want to stay in the circle? What if they both subtly pull for the loyalty of individual members? When one of life's realities pushes your group beyond the feeling of "kindred spirits," you'll discover that every group, every community, is alive, and filled with yeast and fermentation. Dealing with those unavoidable vicissitudes of life can be a rich source of wisdom for the group, or they can blow the group apart. (More on this in Chapter 15.)

Demands from Group Members outside Meeting Times

What about those people who want support and friendship outside the group, who want to know you are committed to them outside of your weekly meeting? What about requests and phone calls in between sessions? The answers to these questions vary among groups and can often be a source of tension and misunderstandings if not talked about openly. Sometimes a participant wants and expects an ongoing friendship and contact outside the group because the circle feels so intense and intimate. Does being in circle together mean that you'll all come to my mother's funeral and take care of me afterward? Does it mean I can ask you to lend me money when I'm short? Will you bring me dinner if I'm laid up in bed with a broken leg?

We would all like to think that we would extend ourselves to someone we know who is in need, but the reality is that coming together for a shared activity doesn't always translate into all-purpose friendship. People who meet each other regularly to train at a fitness gym, or who see each other weekly because they serve a volunteer organization, or who talk often because their kids all belong to the same soccer team, don't necessarily share other aspects of their lives. A wisdom circle draws people closer, but day-to-day friendship isn't automatic. It depends on factors that have to do with other shared interests and availability. Jane and Mary may develop a friendship outside the circle, whereas Jane and Doug may not. Yet within the circle itself, both Mary and Doug are equally focused on Jane and equally supportive of her.

What if you need to leave the group because of outside demands on your time, but you still want to feel a kinship with the members? You may find that severing yourself from the group results in severing yourself from relationship with most of the individuals within the group. It is unfortunately a fact of group life that the group's commitment to you may only be as strong as your commitment to it. You may understand this truth, yet you are still hurt when your expectations of friendship outside the circle are not met. (Of course, there is nothing to prevent you from maintaining friendships outside the group if you are able to do so.)

Most wisdom circles we know of have assumed, but often left unstated, norms about what kinds of support you can and cannot expect. Most members expect that their commitment to their fellow members extends only to the period of the meeting time, not outside the group. That's the unspoken "contract" that people make with each other in most small groups. Your group may be different; individuals may want to be there for each other in an expanded way.

After a number of ongoing meetings, it is useful to ask the group to consider making explicit exactly what "commitment" means. At a minimum, a commitment within a wisdom circle means that you are fully present to everyone inside the circle and that your commitment to members outside circle time will vary on a case-by-case basis. There are no universal guidelines to follow. These are human relationships, and they unfold in small groups in all their complexity, just as they do in every other nook and cranny of human existence.

In any group, the definition of "commitment" will vary as time passes. Initially, our commitment is to the constants and to gathering at certain times. At some point, however, it is inevitable that certain people will ask for more contact with members because they want a community they can count on beyond the circle meetings. And it is precisely at this point that the group can mature, split, or fall apart. The choice is up to each member, and reconciling differing levels of commitment presents a juicy challenge for the group. It is important to remember that as in other relationships, bonds can deepen. Some people give their hearts freely and widely, while others are more private and protective of their feelings and relationships and like them to ripen slowly. For each of us, it's like learning to ride a bicycle: There is no other way to learn community than *to be in community*, gathering by gathering, encounter by encounter, day by day.

Till Death Do Us Part

Here are brief sketches of two groups whose members have committed themselves to their circles for life. The first is a circle to which Sedonia [Cahill] belongs. The second is Cindy [Spring]'s mother's group, which has been meeting monthly for more than fifty-six years. (They have never used a talking stick or opened with a ritual, but they are committed to listening and speaking from the heart, so we have included their story here.)

In 1982 Sedonia gathered together a group of women who came to call themselves the Owl/Eagle Lodge—"owl" for the intention to seek wisdom in the deep, dark, and shadowy places and "eagle" for the high, bright light. Over the years they have explored subjects such as personal histories and life transitions such as births, deaths, divorces, and aging. They've talked about spirituality, and about money. They have all agreed to care for one another in their dying times.

•

Seven women met in a Detroit company named Buhl's that manufactured milk cans and, during World War II, also produced airplane parts. The women worked in the clerical offices and were all about the same age—around twenty years old. They started getting together after Betty got married and decided to call themselves "the Buhl women." After the war all of them became wives and mothers, and they continued to meet at each other's houses. They attended each other's weddings (seven in all) and saw a total of twenty-three children born. In the first few decades, certain subjects were off-limits, such as abortion and religion. Now they are all in their seventies, and the bonding of the group is so strong that they can pretty much talk about anything. They expect to attend each other's funerals.

Commitment Ceremonies

The timing of a commitment ritual is entirely up to the group. Some groups will have one after three months; others may wait for more than a year. It may also happen that some members will be ready to commit to an ongoing circle before others are prepared to do so. As in other partnerships, everyone involved has to feel comfortable with the timing.

When individuals make a commitment to the group to show up for the next year, or to simply keep the group going, they need to have a clear sense of personal priorities and not succumb to group pressure, no matter how subtle. To just go along with the group is unthinking compliance at best and will affect the circle's level of trust and rapport when the lack of shared level of commitment becomes obvious.

When all members feel strongly about their bond, they may wish to hold a simple commitment ritual, consisting of a symbolic act and a statement. Each person might light a candle, or place a valued object into a cloth to form the group's "medicine bundle." Such a ritual serves to remind each person of the group's connection to their lives. Every person clearly states just what it is he or she is committing to, for example, a set of values, attendance at meetings, confidentiality, and/or a vision for the future.

Attending meetings is considered the basic sign of commitment. If someone can only come once in a while, the group needs to ask itself if that is enough. In a circle Sedonia was a member of, another woman was consistently late and held herself somewhat separate and aloof. After some months of such reserved behavior, this woman was asked by two other group members about the nature and depth of her commitment. It was difficult to draw her out on her reasons, but after that she was fully present most of the time. It helps to have our commitment challenged—for it helps us get clear about what we value about the circle and what we want to accomplish for ourselves.

A woman left her group in a fit of anger at one of the other members. She refused to come back and process her feelings, or in any way deal with her anger. This left a terrible rip in the circle that had to be carefully mended over time. The group decided to hold a commitment ceremony. They each promised that if any of them had to leave, they would do it in a formal and conscious manner.

As in a good marriage, commitment needs to be renewed periodically, perhaps once a year, for example, around New Year's. If the group goes through a difficult passage such as the loss of a member or a rift between two members, a recommitment ceremony can be healing. When a new person joins, that's also a good time to reaffirm everyone's commitment as well as celebrate the addition to the group.

Finally, a commitment ritual can signal that the group has reached greater depth. Perhaps the members are ready to be more self-revealing, spend more time in silence, do more elaborate rituals together, or become more a part of each other's daily lives. It is important that every circle ask periodically the following questions: Am I learning something new in this group? Is it still nourishing my soul? What would I have to do to make this circle more meaningful? Where do we want to go from here? Is it time to make this circle more responsive to our needs?

When Someone Is Absent

When you are going to be absent from the circle, always let another circle member know you won't be there and why. You can hold the group in your mind and send it some loving energy, or you can spend some time in silent prayer when you know the circle is meeting. The group may choose to keep open a space for you or to light a candle for you to keep your presence alive in the circle. Charlie [Garfield] and Cindy [Spring] belong to a circle that once held a recommitment ritual on New Year's Eve. One member developed a very bad cold and couldn't come, so they set up a speaker-phone so that she was able to participate. By such means, the fabric of a circle is kept intact and strong. You'll come to recognize that a group is not merely a holding ground for individuals. When someone is missing, the group feels different. Its interpersonal dynamics are altered.

The Benefits of Commitment

"We work out our humanity in the cross-currents of relationships," says philosopher Huston Smith, whose observation pinpoints a major benefit of committing to an ongoing circle. We need a place to publicly acknowledge our aspirations and give voice to our dreams and visions. Our humanity is the result of millions of moments of insight and compassion that we gain daily from direct experience and from hearing about the experiences of others. Our relationships influence how well we respond to suffering and how much of the world's beauty we can absorb.

Our power to heal and transform ourselves is aided by a strong commitment to a caring group. The group acts as a mirror, reflecting back the pain, joy, and determination we have allowed to surface. Members may cry when we cry; they will certainly laugh when we laugh at ourselves.

When there's a high degree of trust in your circle, you might consider the Mirror Exercise. In one of the most powerful circles we, the authors, have ever participated in, we passed around a hand mirror. As we spoke, we looked at ourselves in the mirror and described ourselves in third person: "The person I see is beautiful inside but looking old and tired on the outside . . ."; "The person I see is hurting . . ."; "The person I see is not being truthful to her partner . . ."; and on around the circle. This exercise is not easy. It asks you to speak to yourself about yourself in front of others. It asks you to be very honest about who you see and what you know about yourself. When you make superficial comments, you will know by the expression on your face. If you try this exercise, be kind as well as honest with yourself. Be sure to look for what is good and praiseworthy about the person in the mirror, as well as noting what her or his shortcomings are.

We need more than anything to be seen, known, accepted, and loved as we are. In exchange for commitment, a wisdom circle can offer intimacy to the lonely; nourishment to the spiritually hungry; recognition to the underappreciated; a safe place for those needing to vent anger, fear, and frustration; and strength to those who are trying to push beyond their assumed limits.

I remember one moment in my circle when I was able to do something very difficult: tell everyone how much I needed them. It wasn't just one person I was facing, it was a whole group of people. I was taking a terrible risk of needing them to be in my life, and I said so. I have always been afraid of being seen as "needy," so this was a stretch for me.

We hear a lot about the "lack of community" in our busy lives, but we actually belong to a variety of communities besides our family, through work, school, neighborhood, social interests, spiritual affiliation, and the networks created as a result of raising children. Indeed, some of us belong to too many communities, and our feeling of "lack of community" may stem from too many commitments too shallowly made. None of them may satisfy the need for intimacy and spiritual connection that we can find in the compassionate community of a wisdom circle.

SUMMARY OF CONSTANT TEN:

Commit to an ongoing relationship with the people in your circle so as to engender trust and caring among members. Extend that caring to other people, to the Earth and all her creatures by practicing the capacities developed within the wisdom circle in daily life.

CLOSING THE CIRCLE

As we finish our discussion of the tenth constant, we would like to share with you this meditation:

We pray that each of us finds ways of being in circle that help us touch the mystery and the meaning in the experiences that shape our lives. As we struggle with all the changes in our communities and institutions, and with frustration, despair, and cynicism, may we discover the beauty and power of the circle to heal and renew us. Through ritual may we connect with the Source of Life and know that our shared human experience can bring us closer to the Sacred. We cherish the spirit that dwells within us and that animates our group.

We offer gratitude for the miracle of life and acknowledge that we are all "in this" together, that we are part of a continuum that extends from our furthest ancestors through the generations to come. We believe we have the wisdom we need. Through this circle, may we find guidance within and know the unity of all creation. Through this circle, may we awaken to wonder, awe, reverence, and a sense of participation in the inscrutable mystery of being. May we become channels for the interchange between spirit and matter, part of a creative process that reunites all the separate threads of life into one whole tapestry.

May we help one another find the courage to live the wisdom circle constants, to create the kind of world that honors everyone, including ourselves.

PART TWO
THE WISDOM CIRCLE PROCESS

ELEVEN

Calling the Circle

I'd been wanting to have a circle for about a year and a half, but I didn't know how to get it going. My husband said he would join me. Great! Now there were two of us. We decided to take the plunge and invite a few folks over for New Year's Eve, billing it as a circle and party. About twelve people showed up. The circle started at 8:30 and ended at 11:00, just in time to get the party going before midnight. Six of us have continued. That was three years ago and we're still meeting once a month.

Taking the Risk

Many people write to us—the authors—requesting guidelines for setting up a wisdom circle. They say they have been interested in forming a circle with their friends but don't know how to start one and where to get information about joining one. We've heard from people with a wide cross section of interests and goals. One woman felt a wisdom circle would be a perfect format for her group of wealthy philanthropists to examine their relationship to money. A college instructor wanted to use a wisdom circle to help the staff of a medical school share its concerns about administration and faculty relations. The Women's Forest Sanctuary now holds a monthly wisdom circle to focus its environmental activities. A Japanese vegetarian restaurant in Virginia Beach offers a Wisdom Circles brochure to all its patrons; as a result, two circles have been spawned. A number of consultants in organizational development have indicated they will incorporate wisdom circles into their work. Several Unitarian-Universalist fellowships have adopted wisdom circles for ongoing topic groups. A non-profit agency, short on staff and financial resources, internally disorganized, and whose staff was divided along racial and class lines, asked Charlie to lead a wisdom circle that would help them recommit to their initial mission, serving the health needs of their community.

Here is a small sampling from people who either have requested information or have benefited from the wisdom circle process. Their responses indicate the ever-broadening applications for this format.

The San Diego chapter of Friends of the Institute of Noetic Sciences holds monthly meetings with about two hundred people, and some of us were feeling a need to know each other better. We heard about wisdom circles and decided to try one. We let the membership know, and so many people wanted to be part of the circle that we ended up forming four ongoing wisdom circles.

•

As a social worker who facilitates groups for parents of children with disabilities, I'm interested in how I might apply wisdom circles to my practice.

•

After I experienced a wisdom circle at the conference, I took the form back to my classroom. One of my classes is made up of "remedial" kids, the ones that no one else wants. I have to tell you that those kids love the circle. It's about the only time they will stay quiet and listen to one another. They're taking a keen interest in each other's stories. (We use a fuzzball, not a stick.)

•

I have recently become the manager of a branch office for my company and am using the opportunity to bring spirituality to the workplace. I am keenly interested in trying the widsom circle format at our weekly sales/training meetings.

•

I'm the director of a residential vocation/education facility for young people, ages 16-24. The students come here voluntarily to learn a vocation. Where we miss the boat is working with these young people to explore their spirituality. Perhaps the format will help them (and the staff that work with them) learn methods of communicating with themselves and each other.

•

Two years ago, four friends and I decided to "give back" what nature has given to us. We write letters for Amnesty International, install air pollution monitors for free, and support fundraising events, but the group feels a little flat. I'm not quite sure how to define the problem, but perhaps adding a wisdom circle to our activities would be the juice we need.

•

I have introduced wisdom circles to the Phoenix Shanti Group. The circles bring relief from the everyday stressors that come with working in the HIV/AIDS field, and help us deal with personal issues.

•

I regularly meet with a group of friends to discuss the Course in Miracles. I think the wisdom circle format will help ground us and keep us focused on what we're learning.

•

My husband and I are currently studying mythology and are reading Joseph Campbell's book The Hero's Journey, *with a large group of people. Nine of us are interested in expanding our contact and being more personal with each other. I think the wisdom circle format would be a good starting place.*

•

I am in a program that helps people in recovery from substance abuse. I am sure we could all benefit from adding a wisdom circle to our meetings and in our lives.

•

The wisdom circle sounds like a great way for singles to meet each other. You find out if you share the same values. I like that better than going to singles bars or dances.

•

I've been holding monthly meetings in my home for a year now on the topic of "voluntary simplicity." I think the application of the wisdom circle format will better focus our future meetings and ensure participation by all.

How to Begin

If you are feeling the desire to call the power of the circle into your life, ask yourself three questions:

What is your intention?

Who would you like to be in a circle with?

What is your level of commitment? (i.e., How much effort will you put into starting a circle? How often do you want to meet?)

Your answer to the first question will have a major influence on who responds to your call and how well the group succeeds. The clearer you are with your intentions, the better picture you will communicate to those you ask to join the circle. Most of us have several intentions, not just one, for starting a circle. In general, there are two primary motivations: first, to find kindred spirits with whom to share your visions or concerns and, second, to make some kind of change in yourself, feeling that a group setting is a good place to further that process.

The wisdom circle format also appeals to those already in study groups, support groups, or organizations, who want to "go deeper," improve communication, or collect the wisdom of the individuals to make it more accessible to the whole. Established groups may at times favor some members over others. Certain individuals carry more status and are assumed to have more weighty things to say. A wisdom circle may not eliminate these inequalities, but it can go a long way toward leveling the playing field and making the group members more egalitarian and appreciative of each other's "medicine." Often the wisdom circle format will breathe fresh air into a group that's gone stale or keeps going over the same issues. It can provide a way of renewing the vision and finding new connections among members.

Who Should I Ask to Be in the Circle?

Begin to answer the question "Who should I ask to be in the circle?" by making a list of names. Take time to think about those people you know who can comfortably look within and speak from the heart. At the same time, consider the general aims and focus of the group. Your selection of circle mates can strongly influence the success of the circle. Beginning a circle may be an opportunity for you to reach out to people of other subcultures. Or you may want to populate your circle with people who share a particular focus, such as health professionals, people in recovery from substance abuse, or those interested in refining their spiritual path. You may want a group that consists of all men, all African Americans, all mothers, or people in the same part of the life cycle. Within an organization, you may want to ask those people who take its mission to heart, to form a core group.

During the first meeting, it's important that each person state what his or her intention is for joining the circle. It's also important to state the intentions of the wisdom circle format so that everyone is in agreement about the group's structure and values. You might want to have every invitee read the Ten Constants before the first meeting. We have heard of instances in which the circle convener calls everyone into a wisdom circle, and then one or more people in the group decide they would rather have a study group with a designated leader, or a support group in which people offer one another advice. This can create dissension in the first meeting. The wisdom circle format requires that participants simply witness one another and speak from their direct experience. It also requires that a talking stick (or other symbolic object) be used and that ritual be used to create an environment that invites a feeling of sacred time and space.

What We Recommend

The wisdom circles we know of, and are involved in, meet anywhere from once a week to four long weekends a year. The frequency and length of the meetings are determined by the members' needs. A group of hospice nurses at a university hospital can only afford to meet one hour a month because of their schedules. One circle that Charlie and Cindy belong to meets Sunday evenings once a month. Meeting biweekly is also a popular choice. The Daughters of Eos, a women's support group, take out their calendars at the end of every meeting and schedule the next one based on everyone's availability. This results in gaps of as long as two months between meetings, but this meeting style works well in the lives of these busy professionals.

Group size also varies, but we recommend that an ongoing group be no smaller than three and no larger than ten. You want each person to have an adequate opportunity to participate in a satisfying way. Larger groups encourage "hiding" and allow shy people to stay on the sidelines. Length of meeting time must also take into account the size of a group. With more time, you can accommodate more people. One-time circles, such as for a memorial service or for Earth Day, may last an entire day or more and can be any size that suits the location. Large groups can break into multiple circles.

One of the most popular ways to organize a circle is based on gender. Women's circles abound, and there are a fair number of men's circles as well. If you want a mixed circle, you need to make an effort to balance the membership and avoid having a dominant majority of either men or women. One word of caution: It is sometimes more difficult to attract men than women into a circle. Consider one man's thoughts:

> *I've read that the circle is considered "feminine." What emerges in a circle is what [psychiatrist Carl] Jung called "anima" or soul—the "feminine aspect" of our personalities. But circles are entirely suitable for men. We too need possibilities for growth and healing. The men in my circles have no trouble telling their truths and learning to be empathic listeners. It's a mistake to see the circle as somehow only a woman's domain. After all, what do you think a huddle is? It's not only about football. You can "huddle" about other things.*

For many men, the challenge is to recognize the benefits of mutual support and self-revelation. For women, the challenge more often is believing that you have a voice and that others will listen—to see the circle as a model of empowerment. If you are used to being interrupted by family members or discounted by bosses at work, it may take time to get used to speaking for as long as you care to hold the stick.

Pitfalls and Warning Signs

Those motivated to join wisdom circles are frequently the kinds of folks who see themselves as open-minded and open-hearted. The vision and values embraced by the Ten Constants are about creating a world that works for everyone, but certain people do not, or cannot, subscribe to those values—people, for instance, who feel a certain race or a certain religion is superior to others. Even more challenging to deal with are the people who pretend to share the values of the circle but whose words or behavior belies their claims.

If you put out a general call to begin a circle, you will usually attract people who are genuinely interested in the egalitarian nature of the process. You may also attract some people with deep personal problems who are looking for a place to deal with them or to be rescued in some way. (More on this in Chapter 15.) If you are creating an ongoing circle, it is best to screen as well as you can for the following "red flags":

People with serious psychological problems, who, for example, have severe depression or a

history of violent behavior, or who have made any recent referral to suicide.

People with substance abuse problems that impair their thinking ability and their interactions with other people.

A person with any of these problems will not likely benefit from a group in which mutuality is key. A wisdom circle cannot perform specialized mental health intervention or conduct psychotherapy any more than it can do bypass surgery. There are other personality problems that may indicate that a person is not a good candidate for your wisdom circle:

1. **Excessive narcissism: Talking only about oneself and an inability to engage other people who are talking about themselves.**
2. **Dogmatism: Having a rigid set of political, religious, or philosophical beliefs that eliminate honest inquiry and discourse; needing to filter everything through their version of "the truth."**
3. **Chronic pessimism or cynicism: Having a worldview that disallows any vision of a positive future or holds that civilization is collapsing and that nothing can be done to avert catastrophe (i.e., "all is lost").**

Again, a person who exhibits any one of these characteristics consistently will find it difficult to participate in the open-minded and open-hearted manner that best serves a wisdom circle.

When you are first calling a circle, you may also consider whether to invite someone who is facing a crisis such as receiving a recent life-threatening diagnosis, being the primary caregiver for a loved one who is dying, going through a divorce, or experiencing any major loss. Life events such as these consume the bulk of our psychic energy and may leave little energy available for bonding with the group. Although people vary in their ability to cope with such challenges, a life crisis could become the ongoing topic, with other people's concerns left on the sidelines. On the other hand, such individuals may welcome the chance to get relief and be with people who are not consumed by personal suffering. Of course, a circle can be purposely formed to address a specific crisis. What matters here is what is best for a person facing one. He or she may benefit most by being with others in similar circumstances in a facilitated support group. It is important to note that in an ongoing circle, any or all of these crises are likely to occur in the lives of group members. The circle must be committed to supporting its members during such events. It might also be useful to recommend to the distressed person a support group or help from a professional.

When you are considering people to call for your circle, you obviously want to make reasonable and compatible choices. In general, if you emphasize the particular values and purposes of the group, people will screen themselves. But even with the most careful selection, your group may soon reveal some rough edges. These can either become wedges that keep the group from coalescing, or they can serve as grist for the mill when the group is ready to explore their differences and learn from them.

What Is Your Level of Commitment?

Before you call your circle, decide how much time and energy you're prepared to commit to the group. Getting one up and running may take more than a few phone calls and one meeting. Then there is the question of meeting frequency. You may find that you are ready to meet once a month, whereas a number of people might prefer twice a month or weekly. How much time can you give this process? How much time do you need in between sessions to digest what is said?

Many of us hunger for a serious commitment. Opening up, trusting, and being authentic are all possible with a group of people you know are prepared to devote a good deal of time to the circle and to one another. Still, what counts overall is the quality of exchange that occurs when you do get together. A group that meets monthly, or even quarterly, and engages at deep levels of truth-telling can feel more "committed" than a group that meets weekly but is stuck in "terminal niceness" and manages only a superficial dialogue. You need to consider the question of frequency and pose it to the invitees in the first meeting. It doesn't need to be answered then but may be determined after members get acquainted.

If you have decided to call a wisdom circle, or to introduce the format into an already existing circle or group, you have a responsibility to get the newfound circle off to a good start. Its success will depend on how well you understand the constants and the process and how well you explain them. You could suggest that your group use a talking stick but fail to explain how this acknowledges each speaker and creates a safe container; or you might open the meeting with a ritual, without telling members its significance. If your explanations are incomplete, more than likely you'll end up with people saying: "This feels pretty stiff. We don't really need the ritual," or, "Passing this stick is silly. Let's not do this anymore," or, "Why are we calling in the four directions? Are we lost?" And you will have blown a chance to involve people who might otherwise have been open to the wisdom circle. We suggest that you become thoroughly familiar with the constants before you start so that you can imbue the first meeting with an understanding of these values.

Another Word about Lateness

One issue that comes up over and over again in groups is lateness. Because we open with a ritual that sets a tone for each meeting, everyone must be on time to participate. Chronic lateness often indicates a lack of commitment. If you cannot be punctual for a gathering, it's best to let someone know ahead of time, even if you're going to be just ten minutes late. If you get stuck in traffic or meet with a last-minute delay, it's best to inform people as soon as it is your turn to speak. It may be that the time agreed upon just doesn't work for someone who has children to feed or who often has to work overtime. The group then needs to decide if certain reasons for frequent lateness are acceptable, whether the time needs to be changed, or whether to ask members to attend only those meetings when they can be on time. More than once, the issue of chronic lateness has consumed groups and caused members to drop out.

Money and Wisdom Circles

We founded our organization, Wisdom Circles, with the understanding that its format could be given away free of charge. We send a brochure explaining the Ten Constants to anyone who writes or calls us. We also propose to anyone initiating a wisdom circle the following guidelines about money matters:

- **People using the wisdom circle format in an informal setting (someone's home or community gathering place) should charge no money for the circle.**
- **If a space has been rented, the participants may be asked to make a donation or to divide the cost of the rental equally among themselves.**
- **When we are asked to help lead a wisdom circle for a service-oriented, nonprofit organization, there is no charge. If a nonprofit organization is charging a registration fee for a conference or fund-raiser, or offering a wisdom circle as part of a larger revenue-generating event, it is acceptable to receive an honorarium.**
- **If you are invited to lead a wisdom circle for a corporation, an association, or a profit-making training program, a fee-for-service can be charged.**

We cannot cover all the different circumstances in which money might be a consideration in the offering of a wisdom circle. We want to emphasize that being a wisdom circle maker is a community service, not a way to make a living. In keeping with the spirit of the Ten Constants, holding a wisdom circle is akin to leading a spiritual service or prayer gathering. It is not an entrepreneurial enterprise, but a gift from the heart.

When our human spirit is unleashed, what's unleashed is the prosperity of the soul, the prosperity of the heart, an experience of love, relatedness, inner connectedness, and a deep truth that we are each other. And in that truth, the whole world belongs to you.

—Lynne Twist, in an interview on New Dimensions *radio*

TWELVE

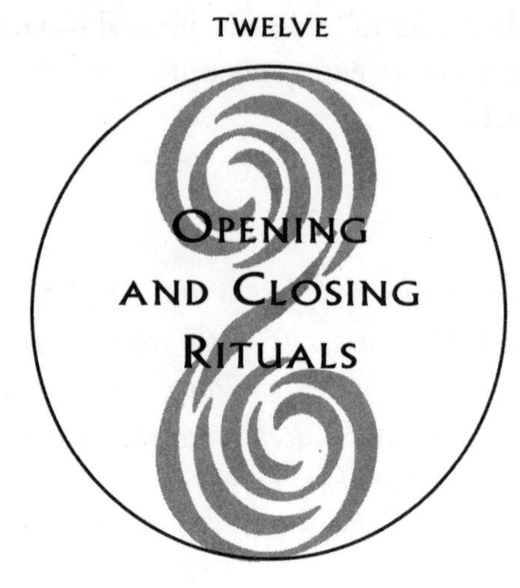

Opening and Closing Rituals

Each one of us has worked hard to cultivate certain qualities—compassion, generosity, humor, caring, centeredness. As we go around the circle, please give voice to a special quality that you bring with you. What "medicine" do you offer us? We don't need you to be modest at this point. Call into the circle the gift you bring that we can count on.

This invocation ritual is one we use often to open a wisdom circle. We ask each person to light a candle as they call in his or her personal quality. Whatever way is chosen to open the circle, the goal is to bring everyone into sacred time and space and to set the activity of the circle apart from the demands of home and work, traffic jams, and unpaid bills—the background noise and central concerns of our "everyday selves." We also use ritual to consciously mark the close of the circle—to complete the experience and honor our time together before we return to daily life.

Invoking the Spirit of Compassionate Community

In her book *Calling the Circle*, Christina Baldwin says: "Rituals were designed to remind us over and over and over again of our true relationship to life: that of a grateful, amazed supplicant at the feet of mystery." Rituals are also key to accomplishing that shift of consciousness from "I" to "We." They are composed of symbolic gestures, shared sensory experiences, movement, and the creation of a special environment. Although we most often use words, they are not essential. You can create a ritual using dance, meditation, silent hand-holding, drumming, and anything else that calls you into the present moment with your whole body, mind, and spirit. We urge you to try several different ways to open your circle. The best rituals provide a simple format, usually consisting of words and actions, that is easy to follow and allows for individual expression. The opening ritual at the beginning of this chapter is an example. At their best, rituals tap into our deeper emotions as they connect us with the sacred. At one circle, a poem by the Czech writer Vaćlav Havel invoked a spiritual dimension. If the ritual you choose doesn't conjure up a feeling such as joy, love, communion, gratitude, reverence, or personal power, then it isn't worth doing.

Remember that the circle maker has a responsibility to create a comfortable and safe space for everyone. Consider carefully the introduction of an unfamiliar form or symbol. Something from a spiritual tradition not known to everyone in the circle needs to be explained. Bring only those rituals into the circle that have meaning for you, ones that you have tried yourself. Painting yellow lines across the forehead may have a powerful meaning in an aboriginal culture, but it may seem weird to a circle of physicians in Chicago.

The ritual needs to create community, not alienate people. Placing a large statue of the Buddha in the center of the circle may be inspirational to those familiar with his teachings. The same gesture might not translate so well for a devout Jewish group. Listening to a tape of the sitarist Ravi Shankar might seem like a good idea to you—but someone who has no affinity for music from India may hear only "noise." You will not create a sacred space with a ritual that seems foreign or bizarre to other members.

Good rituals feed the soul. Be a soulful ritual maker whose offerings nourish your fellow participants. As Hollye Hurst says in "Ritual Revival":

> *Through ritual work, each participant becomes a magician, a shaman and healer with the keen responsibility to maximize human potential by consciously venturing into unexplored realms of the psyche as if mining for gold. By acquiring symbolic fluency through ritual process, participants can gain immediate experience of dwelling in the sacred—unfiltered through gurus, masters, priests or dogma.*

Suggestions for Opening Rituals

For opening rituals, you can choose from any one of the following categories and combine them in creative ways.

- **Invocations**

  The opening statements in Chapters 1–10 are examples. (They are integrated into a single statement invoking all the constants at the end of the book.) You might read a selection from *Earth Prayers* or *Life Prayers*, books edited by Elizabeth Roberts and Elias Amidon, or choose a poem or prayer that has significance for the group and that inspires or sets a meditative tone.

  Each person may invoke a quality such as courage or compassion or call the wisdom of an ancestor into the circle.

- **Symbolic Gestures**

  The most frequently used opening gesture is the lighting of a candle. This may be accompanied by a story or statement to the group, but it can also be done in silence while members make their own internal affirmations. An alternative to candles (especially outdoors) is to pick a stone or other small object such as an acorn out of a basket and place it in the center of the circle.

  Breaking bread and eating from the same loaf is a lovely and ancient ritual—as is the sharing of a meal.

  Members might also bring a treasured object from home, place it in the center of the circle, and explain its significance. Other contributions can be made to the center from a category agreed upon in advance, such as a favorite book, animal figure, or something from outdoors.

- **Other Shared Sensory Experiences**

  Listening to music (The flute compositions of Carlos Nakai work well, as do many classical compositions, such as *Ode to Joy* by Beethoven.)

  Burning sage or other dried herbs

  Drumming

  Holding hands in silence

  Chanting

  Dancing in circle (An easy variation is described in Angeles Arrien's CD *The Warrior*—see the list of Suggested Resources at the end of the book.)

- **Silent Meditation**

  If you open the circle with silent meditation, you might want to use music or an invocation to set the tone. Another possibility is to agree beforehand that everyone will enter the room quietly and sit in silence for a certain period of time.

The Center Table

Mythologist Mircea Eliade says, "Every human being tends, even unconsciously, towards the Centre, and towards his own centre, where he can find integral reality, that is, sacredness." Eliade points out that the concept of a spiritual and geographical "center" was crucial to ancient peoples. Every culture defined the center of its universe—usually a prominent mountain or some extraordinary feature of the landscape. Every ancient city had a center; every building, every home, and each person was assumed to have a "center" as well. This was not necessarily the midpoint of the structure; rather, it was a sacred place—an inexhaustible source, a doorway to a greater metaphysical reality. The "center" is where the essence of the whole exists symbolically.

The physical center of a wisdom circle is generally a cloth or central table, what some may call an "altar." Symbolic objects may be placed on the table by the circle maker. Members of a group might bring articles that represent their special gifts or talents. If the opening ritual invokes our ancestors, each person might put something on the cloth that reminds them of a parent or grandparent. The physical center holds the group together in a special way—it provides a shared visual and aesthetic focus. It also allows a speaker who prefers not to make eye contact to concentrate on something both grounding and meaningful while speaking to the circle.

Our guidelines for the center table are to keep it simple and let it be visually pleasing. Some wisdom circles use this place to honor the four elements that sustain all life: the earth we stand on, the air we breathe, the water that flows through our bodies, and the warming fire of the sun. Symbols of those elements are usually pleasing to everyone. Other objects appropriate to the group can be used as well. Connecting the central table to the seasons is also a popular approach. During a summer solstice circle, the center can be a profusion of colorful flowers. In the autumn, you might gather harvest vegetables and fruits—squash, grapes, persimmons, and pomegranates—and afterward let each person take a piece home.

Items that relate to the meeting's topic or to the group's special area of inquiry are also effective focal objects. Parents of troubled adolescents might put baby pictures of their children on the table to remind them of a time when relationships were simpler. The Women's Forest Sanctuary wisdom circle sets out redwood sticks gathered from the property they're purchasing. A group focusing on their vision for the future might put a pile of acorns or redwood seeds in the center. A group that has chosen mortality and death as their topic might choose an unadorned pot of soil.

The Environment

Where will your circle meet? Wherever you choose to gather, remember that you are creating an environment, an ambience, that needs to be conducive to entering sacred time and space. The lighting should be soft. Make sure everyone can be comfortably seated, either on the floor or on chairs. If you must meet in an impersonal conference room or the back office, do the best you can to soften the room with flowers, candles, an incense stick, or a fragrant potpourri.

Closings

The circle maker who closes the circle needs to develop an intuitive sense of the needs of the group at the end of the meeting. Ask if any members need to express something individually—for instance, make a request for a prayer for something they're facing that week. The closing ritual is an ideal place for fulfilling the intention of Constant Four—expressing gratitude. One way to close the circle is to ask each person to express gratitude for some blessing or teaching received. Another way to close is to ask each person to "make a wish" for himself or herself or for someone close to them, a gesture that goes nicely with the blowing out of the candles lit during the opening ritual. Another suggestion is to affirm a vision or goal that you believe is possible to achieve within your lifetime (or within your organization).

The closing ritual can also honor the group experience. Traditional closings such as group hugs and holding hands can reinforce the group's closeness when they feel appropriate. Many people enjoy singing together. An effective closing also includes a reminder that whatever we learn in circle is "practice" for a way of being in our daily lives.

> *As we move to close this circle and open ourselves to the external world, let us give each other our thanks for our participation and love during this gathering. Let the symbols of fire within our hearts and cooling water in our soul help us as we return to our work. Although we will empty this vessel, we will know each other and whenever we meet we will see ourselves reflected once again.*
>
> —*Larry Yang*

THIRTEEN

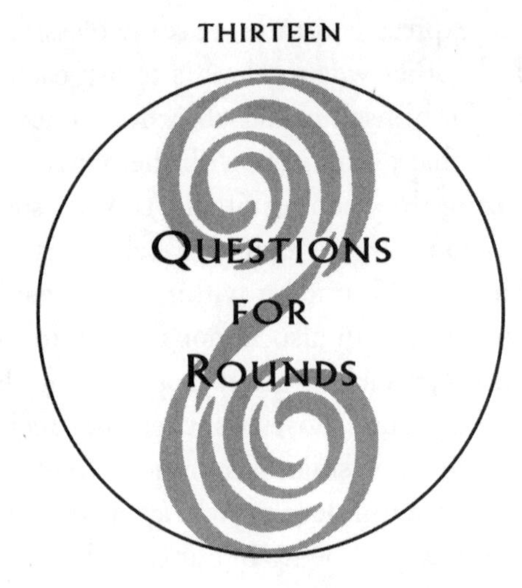

Questions for Rounds

We enter the wisdom circle with a commitment to explore our basic inquiry: How can we continue to survive, dream, hope, and carry on in this time of change and transformation? How can we release rigid patterns of thinking and broaden our perspective? Let's set aside philosophical debate and listen to each other with an open heart. Let's begin by asking provocative questions, questions that push us to reconsider the values and assumptions upon which we base our lives.

Whom Does the Grail Serve?

Two of the most provocative questions of all time are found in the tale of the Fisher King, the most famous of the Arthurian legends. The Fisher King lies wounded for twenty years while everything in the countryside has fallen into ruin. No crops are growing. The kingdom is suffering along with its king, and there seems to be no cure. What everyone is waiting for is someone to ask *the right question*, the question that will spark the healing of the king and therefore of the whole community.

The knight Parsifal rides into the king's castle when he is young and foolish and fails to speak at all. He asks no questions and rides away feeling curiously empty, as though he missed the most important opportunity in his life. Years later, after many trials and adventures, Parsifal rides into the castle again. The land is still in ruin. The king is still in agony. This time, however, there is hope. Parsifal has grown wise and bold, so now he asks two important questions: "What ails thee?" and "Whom does the Grail serve?" The source of the wound has never been addressed, and that is one reason it is lingering. Because it is a spiritual wound, the only thing that can heal its agony is the Grail itself, the chalice used at the last supper by Jesus. To drink from the Grail is to partake in the communion of love that nurtures all people and living things. When Parsifal asks, "Whom does the Grail serve?" he is asking if the king will claim this healing for himself and for the whole community. When the king replies: "It serves the Grail King," he is making a commitment to his own spiritual renewal and pledging to offer this abundance to his people. At that moment, the Fisher King rises from his bed, joyful and healed, and life begins to flourish in the kingdom as well.

It is the right question, asked at the right time, that brings about the healing. In his little book *He: Understanding Masculine Psychology*, the Jungian analyst Robert Johnson retells the story of the Fisher King. He explains that asking the question signals a shift in Parsifal's consciousness. It also alerts us to where the true center of the human personality lies—in the soul. For years both Parsifal and the Fisher King were concerned with their own personal ambitions. Their center was the ego, the "I," and so the answer to them would have been: the Grail, or the love and fullness of life, serves me. By questioning *whom* the Grail serves, Parsifal opens the possibility that there is another center, a larger way of being in the world that serves the fullness of life. This kind of shift in consciousness is momentous: It's akin to a person who's been assuming that the world is flat asking the question, "Could the earth be round?" Just asking the question opens up new possibilities. Johnson says that no sooner has the question been asked, then the answer reverberates through the castle halls: "The Grail serves the Grail King." The true king lives at the divine center. He represents the figure of God or is a representation of the Divine. In Jungian terms, he is the larger Self.

Johnson says this myth is about the journey we must make to find the true meaning and purpose of life. Both the Fisher King and Parsifal had spent years thinking that the aim of life was personal happiness, an aim that proved very elusive. When Parsifal raised the question, "Whom does the Grail serve?" or in simpler terms, "What is the larger purpose in life?" the answer came back clearly that the ultimate aim of life is not the pursuit of personal happiness, but to serve the Grail, or God, or the greater Self through service to the whole. In wisdom circle terms, this is what we mean when we talk about making the shift from "I" to "We." Johnson says it takes time to arrive at this point. "It is humbling," he says, "that we hear of this inner center only when we are ready for it and when we have done our duty of formulating a coherent question." He also points out that Parsifal needed only to ask the question with an open heart. "To ask well," says Johnson, "is virtually to answer." When we ask from our hearts, we enter a new field of awareness, and the point of view or attitude we need is given to us. It grows out of the asking, out of our willingness to surrender to the moment and call upon the larger Self.

Asking the Right Questions

Tell us something about the history of your name—how you got your first name, your last name, or a nickname.

We often use this inquiry to begin the rounds of a wisdom circle as a way of introducing people to each other. Each person reveals something personal about themselves. We've heard an amazing range of answers to that seemingly simple question. One woman, born in Germany before World War II, said she had originally been given a Jewish name, but when her family fled the Nazis and moved to England, she had been given a Christian name so she would "fit in." For years, she told us, she secretly wanted to take back her "real" name.

One man traced the origins of his name back to the fourteenth century. A woman revealed that she really didn't like her name and asked the group to call her Joy instead. A woman of Puerto Rican descent had six names—each one linked to an ancestor who was part of her identity. A man named Miles said that in Latin his name meant soldier or warrior; he had always felt his role was to protect those who could not defend themselves. Some people have never given much thought to their names. A surprising number say they've been burdened their whole lives with names they dislike. A few people, mainly women, have changed their names as a sign of achieving a sense of self, of being their own person.

Questioning something as basic as our names gives us a glimpse of the ways a wisdom circle encourages us to shake up old thinking patterns. We have found that posing provocative questions is one of the best ways to stimulate self-reflection and deep truth-telling. The kinds of questions that best serve us are those that inspire self-reflection and allow us to draw from our direct experiences. Such questions sometimes spark revelations that surprise the speaker. Sometimes they uncover old wounds, and tears come with the answers.

Just as in the tale of Parsifal, the most stimulating questions ask us to see ourselves in a larger context, to see our dreams and our woundedness in a bigger framework that takes into account our relationship with other people. We believe the art of asking the right question is a talent, one that can be developed. In Chapter 2, we gave some general guidelines for formulating questions. Now we want to give you some that we've found particularly effective in jump-starting a group. Because there are so many different kinds of issues that a wisdom circle can address, we have listed the questions by generic categories.

Envisioning the Future for Yourself, the Group, the Community, or the Next Generation

- What vision do you have for yourself, your family, your organization?
- How does your current situation compare to your vision?
- How optimistic are you that your vision can be realized? What is helping and what is hindering you in realizing your vision?
- What makes you feel powerless to make changes? What encourages you to move forward and make the changes that are needed?
- What is the most personally exciting commitment you will make toward building a fulfilling future for yourself, the group, etc.?

Healing Wounds and Working toward Wholeness

- What happened to hurt you, and what do you need in order to heal?
- What keeps you going despite your wounding?
- Recall an event or period in your life that was particularly painful. Allow your wisest self to guide you as you answer this question: "What important life lesson came from this time that you might regard as a gift?"
- Tell us a healing story from your own experience.

Learning More about Ourselves

- Tell us something you're proud of. This can be something you received recognition for, or something that no one knows about except you. Please *do not* be modest (insisting, for example, "I was only a small part of the effort," "anyone else could have done it," etc.).

- Tell us about an act of courage or about a transformative experience in your past. How was this a watershed event in your life? How did it change you?
- Complete this thought: "I always thought I'd like to . . . (describe an activity), but I can't because. . . ." (This wonderful question from author Barbara Sher challenges us to name our perceived limitations.)
- Complete this thought: "If I were sure you were all listening from the heart, I would tell you about. . . ."
- What did you want to be when you grew up? What happened to that dream?
- Describe an important cyclical event in your life and why you value it (e.g., an annual vacation, menstrual cycle, Christmas, full moon, birthday).
- Tell about a time in your life when you were really scared (when you were in physical danger, or a loved one was threatened in some way). How did you get through it? What did you learn about yourself?
- What makes you angry? Why?
- Is there anyone whom you consider to be a role model or teacher? If so, who and why?
- If there was one question whose answer would bring you great fulfillment in life, what would it be?
- Do you have a haven or special place where you feel spiritually nourished? Where a positive experience is almost guaranteed? Describe this place, and tell us why you are so drawn to it.
- Now that I am (give age), this is what is up for me. (This question is especially good in a circle with a broad age range.)

- What do you have faith in?
- What do you think will happen to you when you die?
- What people are you deeply grateful for in your life? Why? What would your life be like if they suddenly vanished?
- What emotional baggage are you carrying? What old anger, hatred, jealousy, feeling of inferiority? What would help you to let it go?
- What's workin' ya? What's learnin' ya?

Exploring Our Differences

- In what ways are we humans alike? How do we differ from one another?
- What is a basic assumption you hold about why things are the way they are?
- What types of people do you feel superior to? inferior to?
- How is daily life different for the person who gets up every morning feeling part of the "majority" of his or her society, as opposed to someone who gets up every day feeling stereotyped or marginalized by that society? Which person do you identify with?
- What does "honoring cultural diversity" mean to you?
- What attitudes toward people from other races or ethnic groups did you inherit from your parents and other ancestors? (This question, which has provoked many healing discussions among people from different races, was given to us by author Nancy Thompson.)

Witnessing Each Other's Lives

- Tell us one of the most important things you have learned so far about how to live life.
- What courageous step do you most need to take right now in your life? What people and circumstances are most supportive? Most hindering?
- What is sacred to you? Why?
- What makes you extremely sad? Why?
- What makes you extremely happy? Why?
- What is your relationship to money?
- If you had no need to generate an income, where would you put your energy?

Getting Acquainted

- Tell us something about the history of your first or last name or nickname.
- What drew you to this wisdom circle? What about this way of gathering appeals to you?
- Tell us an aphorism, a quote, or recite a poem that gives you strength and inspiration. Or share a piece of personal wisdom you draw on in daily life.
- Which of the Ten Constants do you feel the most affinity with? the least?
- Do you have a special tree or animal that you have deep reverence for? Why?

Questions for Organizations

- What work have you done recently that you're most proud of?
- Which of our (organization, team) accomplishments excites you the most?

- Can this organization be a place for you to find yourself and serve your community? How?
- What has heart and meaning for you in this work?
- What gifts do you bring to this work?
- How does this work fit into your life?
- How does your personal life support your work? How does your work pull energy away from your personal life?
- Do you see inconsistencies between what the organization says its values are and what you do on a daily basis?
- Tell a story of when you learned something vital about how to do your job from a client, customer, or patient.

QUESTIONS FOR ACTIVISTS

- What is motivating you to commit to this cause? Use images, and be as specific as possible.
- What needs of yours get met through this commitment?
- How much of your personal life, family relationships, and health are you sacrificing for this commitment?
- How often do feelings of hatred well up in you? despair? satisfaction? success? Why?
- How often do you find yourself in an "us versus them" mentality? How often do you recognize the "enemy's" traits or shortcomings in yourself?

Going for a Deeper Experience of Life

- Who are you really? What do you see when you drop the mask and look beyond the persona?
- Who are you beyond all the roles you fill?
- How would you choose to die?
- What are you most looking forward to in old age? Most afraid of?
- Talk about the death of someone else that has, or will, fundamentally transform your life.
- What racial, ethnic, sexist, ageist, etc., stereotype do you hold that you wish you could erase from your mind?
- What does it mean to you to be "a full woman"? "a full man"?

Closing-Round Possibilities

- Tell us something you want to remember from this wisdom circle.
- Offer a prayer, a benediction, a closing thought.
- Offer gratitude for a blessing in your life.
- Tell someone in the group what you most appreciate about them.
- Make a wish for yourself, or for this community, or for the earth.

We recommend that your circle focus on one topic or on a set of related questions per meeting. It's often best to pose a question and suggest that members close their eyes for at least thirty seconds to see what responses arise "from the bottom of the lake." A round is complete when each person feels satisfied that she or he has spoken to the topic, responded to the question, or chosen to pass. Some circles adopt the practice of making sure everyone has had the opportunity to speak once before anyone speaks a second time. Someone's response may trigger an interest in a related topic. Be sure that everyone who cares to has spoken to the question at hand before suggesting a new one.

Alternatives to Questions

Questions aren't the only way to spark rounds in a wisdom circle. As we suggested earlier, you can use a poem, listen to an audiotape or CD, or watch a video segment as the springboard to deep sharing in a circle. Guided-imagery exercises and visualizations can lead you into deeper truth-telling and self-inquiry. Sometimes questions aren't necessary because circle time is used for people to share what is most pressing for them at the moment. Chapter 16 gives a variety of suggestions for special occasions that can be celebrated with wisdom circles, including rites of passage and milestone anniversaries.

In searching for the best ways to deepen the experience of a wisdom circle and to stimulate learning, keep looking for bigger questions. Choose Grail-serving questions, not solely self-serving ones. Good questions challenge everyone to think, to feel, to examine, to change. The best responses come when we reconcile head and heart. Remember that you do not have to rehearse your responses. You'll discover new things in the power of the moment. Remember that you can hold the stick, allow silence to enter the circle, and wait for something to percolate from deep inside yourself. When you come together in a caring, supportive group, you tap into something larger than your own personal consciousness. Insights and feelings can flow through you and express themselves in words that may astound you. As the poet Rilke reminds us, not every question has an answer, but our quest requires that we *ask*.

> *Be patient toward all that is unresolved*
> *in your heart and try to love the questions themselves*
> *like locked rooms and like books that are written in*
> *a foreign tongue. Do not now seek the answers. . . .*
> *Live the questions now.*
>
> —*Rainer Maria Rilke,* Letters to a Young Poet

FOURTEEN

Sustaining the Process

A little yeast transforms a great amount of flour and water into beautiful loaves of bread. What a miracle! Perhaps even a small amount of time spent in a wisdom circle can be the yeast that gives rise to love and spirit, self-acceptance, and service and begins to transform our lives. As we gather, we celebrate our interdependence, give thanks for our gifts and for our connections to each other. May this profound feeling of trust and stewardship extend beyond our circle and encompass the earth.

Our ideal for wisdom circles is that they become the yeast that animates our lives, and we hope to sustain that feeling of aliveness in the larger context of our lives. We may become aware of new feelings and deeper ways of being in relationships. In other words, something within us awakens, and life in our wisdom circle suggests a new norm for all our relationships. More authentic, more connected, more alive to possibility.

Cultivating that aliveness, that vitality, is the central task of a wisdom circle. You can make it a place where each person's wisdom and compassion can be amplified. Then your wisdom circle will become more than a nice place to meet and get support—from which you come away feeling more secure or "stroked." It will become a practice arena for daily life, a place to learn to speak and listen—learn that we are capable of speaking and listening from our hearts. Extending that way of being outside the circle is the work. In time we may begin to offer wisdom and compassion more often to those around us as we become the yeast that helps foster change within our environment.

An Oasis of Possibility

So much of our days are filled with fear and insecurity. We grow numb to suffering in the world. We're filled with denial about how bad things are in our cities, in the environment that surrounds us. We have a growing sense of being lied to and manipulated by advertising, politicians, and the media. We are aware of the discrepancy between what is and what could be in our relationships. When we participate in a wisdom circle, we feel relieved for a moment of our sense of hopelessness about these problems and our seeming powerlessness in solving them, because we now have kindred people who share our commitment to make some change, however small. The real blessing of a wisdom circle is felt when the loving ways you experience yourself and your relationships with other people are extended outside the circle. But that feeling of aliveness, that more authentic way of being, needs conscious caretaking.

Imagine a bare room—four plain walls, a ceiling and floor, all very nondescript. Now in the center of your bare room imagine a small table with a crystal vase and a most exquisite flower. A rose with petals of red and pink surrounding a golden yellow center. Hold the image of your room with this gorgeous flower in the middle.

What happened? The lifeless room was transformed by the presence of the flower. Was it simply the addition of a colorful element into an otherwise empty environment? No, a plastic toy from K-Mart would not have had the same effect. The flower's beauty fills the room with its presence. It exudes aliveness. What prevents us from being like the flower as we transmit our aliveness out to those bare walls of our world every day?

I really like myself when I'm in my weekly wisdom circle. I like what I say, I like how I am with the other people. It feels good to hold the values of the circle. But it's not so easy for me to take the ways of speaking and listening in the circle into my daily life. There's so little support at work, for instance, for speaking from the heart. I want to know that who I am in the wisdom circle is who I am *in every context.*

•

For me, this wisdom circle has been a place to learn to trust my inner source of guidance. Every time we meet I have more confidence to say what's true for me and to allow that to come from a deeper place within me. The irony is that the more I'm able to "speak my truth," the more what I say reflects how much I care about what's happening to all of us, not just me.

•

Where do you get to talk about racism with people of other races? It's scary for a white person to be in a group where African Americans and Latinos talk about how they've been insulted and discriminated against because of the color of their skin. When I discovered that I wasn't going to be blamed for all the sins of white people, I was able to relax and really listen from my heart. It changed my relationships with people of color outside the circle. I feel more connected than separate.

•

I see a wisdom circle as a place to conduct the struggle for a more meaningful life. There's nowhere else in my life where I can be as honest about what makes me unhappy—mainly my work—and talk about what I'd really like to be doing. Sometimes when I'm at work, I think about the group and how I'd respond differently to my boss, for instance, if they were watching me.

•

My men's group, which consisted of both homosexual and heterosexual members, held a long round on the need for love and affection. Afterward I commented, "Straight men have a lot to learn from gay men about matters of the heart."

•

A circle is a good place to face the gaps in your life, that is, the realities of your existence versus the visions you hold for improvement. I use my women's wisdom circle as a test of my own ability to say what's truly happening in my relationship with my husband and how I'd like things to be. I can only do that because I absolutely trust the commitment to confidentiality that we all took.

•

The beauty of a wisdom circle for me has been finding greater significance in my life experiences, and discovering that other people can actually benefit from hearing how I managed a specific challenge. This has given a greater meaning to my life—I count, my experiences count! I doubt that I'd ever have known that without the process of the circle.

Sustaining the Individual

The most memorable wisdom circles are those in which you come away with greater self-acceptance and self-respect because the group process helped you to know yourself better. Do you feel more empowered, have a clearer vision of your life and how you fit into the larger picture, a better sense of what your unique medicine is, after you have attended a wisdom circle? Did you have the opportunity to reaffirm what you truly value? Did you experience some relief when you revealed your struggle in the company of kindred spirits? Did you grow in your capacity to listen from the heart? Each of these questions suggests an experience that is possible in circle.

To me a wisdom circle is a form of "spiritual practice," which means getting to know myself more deeply. "Spiritual" to me also does not mean stiff or solemn. I like circles that are irreverent, and where we all have a lot of fun—where there's room for anger and all kinds of feelings. I wouldn't stay a minute in a circle if I thought I had to be pious. It would bore me. It's about getting pushed and challenged that makes it a spiritual practice for me.

Yes, a wisdom circle is a place for self-discovery, for nurturing ourselves. And yes, a wisdom circle encourages us to engage the world. It is a place to build a compassionate community and forge a new strategy for living in a world that works for everyone. It helps us reconcile our inner development and our work in the world, not choosing one priority over the other. People who have taken the time to "work on themselves" have frequently compiled an impressive list of workshops, books, retreats, and vision quests. These folks might be called "inner-focused." They believe that the most compassionate and meaningful thing you can do for others is to work on yourself. Others have spent their time doing volunteer work, organizing political and social activities, restoring the environment, and raising children. These are the folks we might call "outer-focused," and they believe the most compassionate and meaningful thing you can do is to try to improve the world. Some of us have done a little—or a lot—of both.

The strengths of inner-focused individuals often center on the ability to be introspective, to get in touch with their feelings, and to understand their healthy motivations as well as those that result in behaviors they would rather not engage in but do, anyway. They know their talents and limitations. The strengths of outer-focused individuals often have to do with their ability to get things done, collaborate, act in support of those who are marginalized by society, and "sustain their gaze" on the suffering of others and not turn away. Wisdom circles are attracting both inner- and outer-focused people. We are learning a great deal as we watch each other attempt to reconcile inner and outer realities.

We feel more sustained as whole human beings when our internal and external environments are in harmony. Ignoring our connections and responsibilities to the world limits us to the narrow confines of our daily lives. We need to see ourselves more broadly as threads in a tapestry. When we do, our sense of isolation lessens. If you have spent your time caring for other people, volunteering to teach literacy to kids at risk, working at a food bank, or lobbying for equal rights for gays and lesbians, you may have gained some understanding of your own wounds and deeper aspirations. Similarly, the self-exploration stimulated by the questions in a wisdom circle can take you into less familiar territory and heighten your capacity for inner guidance.

When we are anchored by an inner reality, a vision, and values we have come to know as our spiritual home, we can "move mountains." In a wisdom circle, cross-fertilization occurs between "inner" and "outer": between our own inner guidance and wisdom, and the experience of others. An integration of the two can enhance our personal development and foster a capacity to be more effective in the world. We are guided by a reconciling question that informs our lives: "Is it viable to the self and workable in the world?"

During the circles Sedonia leads on vision quests, she has listened to stories from many people who find the courage to leave unsatisfying work for something more fulfilling. Mary made the decision to leave her job as a computer analyst and eventually become an environmental engineer. Otto made a commitment to go to massage school, even though his high-tech job promised more security. James made plans to offer classes in spirituality to stretch himself beyond his role as a yoga teacher. Bob was a highly paid lawyer who became an animal rights activist. For the inner-focused, the challenge is to align a wise choice of work in the world with your deeper needs and values. For the outer-focused, the challenge is to take the time to allow that "still small voice within" an opportunity to show up, to be heard, and to inform your work.

When I was part of the "movement" in the 1960s, I was very involved in fighting racism, ending the Vietnam War, and helping to promote a feminist consciousness. I didn't have any time for myself. It was all about the cause. You got by on coffee and doughnuts and didn't think about your health or your living situation because to do so would have taken away from the work. Having lived in that mental state, and then afterward spent years studying Eastern philosophies and meditation, I've seen both sides of it. It's clear to me now that you bring a stronger, more effective person to your activism the more you work on yourself. Not to work on yourself means you let old unresolved emotional and psychological baggage get in the way. And it does, it creates interpersonal problems. I realize now that the more I know myself through this circle process, the more effective I am as an activist.

Sustaining the Group

You know when a circle is working well and when it is not. Sometimes you may have a gut feeling: This is not working for *me*, although it seems to be making everyone else happy. At that point we recommend that you give voice to your discontent.

I'm hearing everyone in this circle do some version of "us 'n them," and it's making me uncomfortable. Yes, the doctors and the administrators have more power than nurses, but I don't think we're going to get very far if we stay at the level of a gripe session. What are we as nurses going to do to get attention focused on patient care?

You may be the "voice in the wilderness" that ultimately brings a clearer understanding into the circle, or you may find that your comments get no support. It is up to you whether to persist in conveying your perspective. Try to stay open to the comments of others, listen from the heart. You can't bludgeon people into seeing things your way, but well-timed observations offered with compassion for the needs stated by others may facilitate the group's maturation. As a last resort, you may decide that there isn't a fit between you and the rest of the group.

What happens when the circle isn't working for most everyone in it? It's time to blow the whistle and make the *process* the content of the circle: "Something feels wrong with the way things are going here." As the group continues, you may find your comments becoming more astute: "It seems every time a difficult or potentially divisive issue comes up, we retreat into 'make nice' and don't really wrestle with it." Or, "I really need to say some heavy stuff tonight, and I'm not sure I trust the group's ability to listen to me and bear witness to my struggles." (This idea was discussed in Chapter 9 and will be amplified in Chapter 15.)

What are the healthy practices that keep a wisdom circle in good shape? The nutrients that sustain the group over time? Here is a checklist for your wisdom circle as it matures:

Does the group always open and close with a ritual? Without *temenos*—a sacred container—you do not have a wisdom circle. You may have a great discussion circle, or support group, but not a wisdom circle.

How does the content of the circle get chosen? Do one or two people make the choice every time? A wisdom circle addresses the needs of every individual, and while this may not be possible every time, there must be a sense that everyone's needs are met over the course of several meetings.

Consider a periodic "safety check" to take a reading on the group. Is anyone uncomfortable or inhibited by the way things are going? If so, why?

If you feel that people are not listening to you, that someone is judging you, or that others can't wait to have their turn, the circle loses its power to bear witness to your life. Have a round on the question "How well are we listening?"

If the group consistently feels "there's not enough time," then lengthen the meeting or increase the frequency. Perhaps the group is too big and two groups need to form. Mitosis (the splitting of one cell into two) is a naturally occurring phenomenon.

If your group makes little room for silence, try building it in, right after the opening ritual. Allow for two or three minutes of meditation or silent prayer. Does your group allow enough "space" for people to assimilate each other's stories? Do you pause after something particularly moving has been said?

Has one person taken over the role of facilitator? Or is everyone making comments about the group's process at one time or another? Sometimes a simple observation such as, "I'm having a hard time staying tuned in to this round," or "Did anyone else find what Jean said hard to understand, besides me?" can revive a tired circle.

Check in on how each person is trying to live the values of the wisdom circle in daily life. Try this topic for a round: Tell of an instance when the group empowered you to take a risk and act with more integrity. Such stories strengthen the group and demonstrate the power of the circle even when you are not together.

Other Tips on Sustainability

Sometimes a group can give greater legitimacy to suffering and pain than to joy and happiness. Joy is something we remember once in a while, usually when somebody says, "Hey, we haven't talked about the things that are working, the parts of our lives that are going marvelously well." It seems there's a covert validation of the painful experiences: loss, death, abuse, woundings of various sorts. We think that's the real stuff, and often we forget our joyful moments, our heart connections with other people.

Just as we are sustained by a special event every once in a while such as a birthday party, so too are wisdom circles sustained. In Chapter 16 we will suggest a variety of one-time ceremonies that deepen the bonds of circle members. The group may want to turn over the entire meeting to one member's significant loss such as the death of a parent or a divorce or loss of a job. You might also consider an extra meeting on a solstice or equinox, or to celebrate a major birthday, such as turning fifty.

> *The Daughters of Eos is a group of seven women all in the menopausal period of their lives. As each woman turns fifty, a ceremonial circle is held to honor her. The other six women in the group each write a letter, a page or two in length, that describes what she has learned from and what she admires about the person turning fifty. Each woman lights a candle as she reads her letter from the heart. The letters are collected and put into a beautiful container and given to the birthday person.*

Ongoing groups find they have to adjust for the changing needs of members. People's commitment to the circle may be affected by the birth of a child, a job change, and major loss. A common adjustment is to change the number of meetings—gathering bimonthly instead of weekly, for example. Another common adjustment is to allow members to be absent whose work takes them out of town frequently. Author Sam Keen belongs to a men's group that has been meeting for more than twenty years. Sam had to excuse himself from many meetings when his book *Fire in the Belly* was on the bestseller lists. The "Buhl women," Cindy's mother's group which has met monthly for more than fifty-six years, has adapted to members' changing needs. In her retirement years, for example, Betty leaves Michigan each winter to spend time in a motor home with her husband traveling in the South. She is welcomed back to the group each spring.

Certain very practical considerations also help sustain the circle. Can a member leave to go to the restroom? Of course, but preferably between speakers, if possible. As one circle member remarked, "Freud said that biology is destiny, so we'd better learn to have compassion for our bladders."

In longer circles that last all day, take time for meditation breaks and some exercise, such as stretching. Some members find they like to have time to assimilate something from the circle (thoughts, comments, emotions, etc.) by taking a walk or writing in a journal. Suggesting such a break can be a welcome co-facilitation comment on the circle process.

Sustaining Others

One very positive way to enhance the aliveness of your circle is to help others start their own. Allowing your circle to be a resource for others gives an added sense of purpose to the group. Sedonia's Owl/Eagle Lodge has held over a dozen large drumming circles for women to educate them about circles, to exchange circle lore, and to assist women in starting their own. Cindy offers to co-lead an initial circle for groups forming in the San Francisco area. Charlie has seeded wisdom circles in a number of AIDS agencies around the nation and provides guidance to other service organizations starting circles for caregivers.

After experiencing a wisdom circle, you may want to introduce the format to co-workers or into an activist organization. How wisdom circles are presented in a given context depends on what communicates best in that organization. It's important to frame the process appropriately when you introduce the wisdom circle in groups of goal-directed people such as those working in corporations. If you call it a spiritual practice, you'll often end the meeting right there. Let the discussion evolve organically. Introduce wisdom circles as a place for empowering individuals and strengthening the whole. Focus on deep truth-telling. If you are able to create a safe enough container, someone will likely say, "I can't believe I'm talking about such difficult things as comfortably as I am. I've never felt the permission or the safety to talk so honestly before."

You might then take a turn and say, "What kind of development do you think we're talking about here?" Somebody will offer a comment about the importance of having meaningful work and how difficult it is to integrate their work lives with their personal values or about the challenge of meeting personal needs while maintaining a commitment to a cause. If you choose to, you'll be talking about spiritual needs in terms most everyone feels comfortable with.

Before you seed new circles, be sure you are well grounded in the process and have taken the constants to heart. You need to *become* yeast before you can *be* yeast in the world.

FIFTEEN

When Coming "From the Heart" Is Hard to Do

Call to mind a person you love dearly. You want this person to be safe and happy and filled with peace. Now think of someone whose behavior irritates you, someone it's hard to extend lovingkindness to. You may want to label this person's behavior as arrogant, or ignorant or neurotic or worse. Now, wish this *person safety and happiness and peace. In this person are gifts that can heal the world. He or she may need to be freed from fear or loneliness or pain in order to bring forth their gifts. Pray that this person, whose words and acts may be hard medicine for you, live a life that is peaceful and full of beauty.*

"May all beings be happy" is a basic tenet of Mahayana Buddhism, practiced in much of Asia. At its core, it contains a profound wisdom—that the highest spiritual attainment is compassion for all beings. The teaching doesn't say, "May all beings that I like be happy," or "May all beings who are nice and sensitive be happy." No, the teaching explicitly states: May *all beings* be happy. Finding that place of lovingkindness, as it's often called, is a spiritual task, and we have the opportunity to develop that capacity in a wisdom circle.

What do you do when you find it difficult to listen from the heart? When you find yourself shutting down and not giving a particular individual your understanding, your patience, or your healing presence? What can you do when you realize that you are mentally invalidating another group member, labeling him or her a "difficult person" rather than trying to see what he or she needs?

There is no doubt that some people's behavior can be challenging to other circle members. Here are examples of some of the most common complaints:

> *I felt Frank was lecturing me as if he were the resident guru. He wasn't talking about his own experiences or feelings, he was pontificating, and I didn't know how to handle it.*

•

> *Marjorie was using the group as a sort of soapbox for her political views, and we were a captive audience. Some people stopped coming for that reason.*

•

> *How do you tell a person they're no longer welcome in the circle? Many of us felt that way about Jim because of his sexist and off-color remarks, but our circle couldn't deal with that. We either shoved the discussion under the rug or made excuses why we couldn't come. Eventually, the circle died.*

•

Janet and Marcy come dragging in and don't have any energy. They expect to get a shot of energy from the group. They don't realize that they can bring the energy of the entire group down—to their level. Sure you're going to be tired sometimes, but that shouldn't be your usual way of being in the circle.

•

I don't like it when Jerry doesn't show up and doesn't take the time to let anyone else know. We have a closed group with a commitment to be there. There are no "drop-in's." When we don't know what's going on, it makes a hole because you think he's coming. You're counting on him. Some people don't realize that what they do has an impact.

•

I get frustrated when the group gets competitive. I was in a circle with four other men, and we knew each other very well and cared about each other. I thought: "Now I'm safe. There won't be any competition here." I soon realized how naïve that was. Almost every time I spoke, the same man would follow me with his comments. He was very invested in being seen as "insightful." It was the old male competitive stuff. One of the other men finally pointed it out, and we discussed our feelings about competition and our needs for intimacy.

A listing of irritating behaviors could be endless, because each one of us responds to some behavior from another person that "pushes our buttons." Then we identify that person as a problem or a difficult person. The behaviors mentioned above would probably annoy most everyone in the group. But when certain behaviors are irritating to some and not to others, that gives us a clue that our own bias may be involved in the assessment. In other words, we may be reacting to another person's behavior in part because of the actual behavior and in part because the behavior triggers associations with negative experiences we've had in the past. The association may be with a domineering parent, or a tardy husband, or an abandonment by a loved one. Most often, we're not aware of these associations when we find ourselves getting upset by someone else.

For some, it's the dominating member who talks too long who is most irritating, or else the quiet member who needs to be drawn out and thus often elicits caretaking by other members. The resident guru can charm some people, whereas others are put off by his know-it-all tone and his "one right way." The contrarian member can hold a group hostage by disagreeing with any suggestion and thus stymie a consensus on how the group can proceed. How do we address these personalities and our own reactions?

What "Difficult People" Can Teach Us

Rather than offer a "solution" or response to each of the situations described earlier, we propose the following guideline: Monitor your thoughts and feelings and observe your participation in circle. You may find yourself thinking of the domineering person as an egotist and mentally and emotionally bypass her. You may endure her comments and let your usual empathy resurface in response to another person's remarks. The opportunity to learn about co-facilitation and mutual responsibility is part of the domineering person's contribution, albeit an unintentional one, to the circle. Similarly, the resident guru teaches us to be wary of absolutism, rigidity, and inflexible certainty in our positions and beliefs. He challenges us to keep our hearts open and teaches us that there is often more wisdom in being open about our fears and uncertainties than in "being right."

A person who takes a consistently adversarial position also teaches us how important collaboration really is. By reflexively standing outside the group, insisting on her own way, the contrarian shows us the significant difference between the thoughtful member whose heart is open to the group when she takes an oppositional stance and the intransigent person who simply must have her own way. When one or more members point out to the contrarian how her comments thwart the circle's process and ask her instead for constructive ideas, such feedback is often enough to get the group back on track again. A visionary can demonstrate the creativity and courage necessary to suggest new directions for the circle, whereas the contrarian simply says "no."

The perpetually quiet member teaches us how quickly people can get lost in circle and in the world and how easily people can move toward invisibility, outside the common concern. In a wisdom circle, members share a heightened awareness of the need for each member's voice to be heard. Attempting to "rescue" such a person is much less useful than a clear, heartfelt comment: "Carmelita, I've noticed how seldom you offer your feelings and stories in the group, and I wonder what we can do to make it more comfortable for you to do so."

We can all empathize with the person who is quiet because of discomfort with self-disclosure. A circle of about twenty people, attended by one of the authors, included a nationally known author who had written a fine book on interdependence and our need to see ourselves as part of the ecosystem. This man was very visibly nervous about being in the circle. He was accustomed to giving lectures to groups of colleagues and students and would have readily spoken about his theories to the group if he had been asked. However, he knew the understanding was to speak from direct experience and chose not to talk for the entire circle. The group members understood his reticence and respected his choice to remain silent.

Guidelines for Responses

As co-facilitators, circle members share responsibility for staying aware of the ways the group tends to shut down. Letting this happen routinely erodes our capacity to be a compassionate community. Rather than resorting to techniques or to ways to "fix the problem," wisdom circle members need to stay close to the constants. Listening and speaking from the heart will go a long way toward creating a milieu in which problem behaviors can be addressed, and everyone learns something from the process.

As your circle matures, you will find yourself asking, "What does our group's process teach us about the nature of the relationships?" How can we grow as a group *and* as individuals through the tough meetings in which "niceness" is not a predominant feature?

We focus first on our own reactions, and eventually we find ourselves reaching out to the person who "presents" the challenge to the group, who some may be labeling a "difficult person." We don't defend or attack the person, but speak our truth and reflect as heartfully as we can to the other person what we hear him saying or see her doing that seems discordant with the group's intentions. For instance, in addressing the "guru's" tutorial style, you might say, "Frank, I really learn from your ideas, and I'd also like to learn what other people are feeling about this topic." Often, this is all that needs to be said.

A comment such as "I don't feel like I'm getting the support I need" is fine when it accurately reflects a member's state of mind. When it becomes the common refrain from one person, however, it can signal the desire for a "rescue mission" and bring down the group if the problem is not dealt with honestly. The balance of speakers' comments in a wisdom circle should favor the topics agreed upon, rather than the group's process unless a process dynamic or difficulty is confusing or disturbing to a member.

The group itself is a living, social organism with the capacity to cope with many different kinds of personalities and with the ability to correct its course, learn, and change. Here are some general guidelines for dealing with those challenging moments:

1. Check your own feelings:

What am I feeling about this person? this incident? the group?

Am I reacting by feeling tense? angry? withdrawing?

Do I frequently blame the other person for his or her beliefs or behaviors and see him or her as the cause of difficulties, when the problem may be a relationship issue between two or more people? Could it be that I and/or some other person are also part of the problem?

Am I trying to understand the person "from the inside," empathically?

Do I acknowledge small positive changes on the other person's part—signs of addressing the problem—or do I expect a complete change of behavior?

Am I willing to stand by this person *and* consider the group's welfare at the same time? Am I willing to be the one person who tries to understand what he or she is going through?

Am I assuming that the other person must change—rather than the group and certainly not me?

My buttons get pushed when someone is very inarticulate, just grasping at ideas, doing stream of consciousness and speaking in partial sentences and incomplete thoughts. I get frustrated trying to find the gist of it and I find myself wishing the person would stop talking. Staying in that place of listening from the heart is a real challenge for me then, probably because there's something in me that's afraid of being inarticulate, afraid of being seen as "not having my thoughts together." At that point, I try very hard to remind myself that this is my practice for listening from the heart.

2. Check the situation of the "challenging" individual:

Is the person acting out of character, or is her or his behavior fairly typical?

Was the problem behavior triggered by a particular incident?

How aware of the problem do you suppose this person is? Domineering members may not be aware of their need to control things, and resident gurus may want validation for being intelligent. Someone who frequently plays victim, always at the mercy of life's circumstances, undoubtedly feels this woundedness outside the group as well. What support can the group offer while at the same time encouraging this person to discover the deeper meaning of the events in her or his life?

What do you suppose the group looks like to the person with the problem behavior? Hostile? Friendly? Nurturing? Judgmental?

Does the person seem so engrossed in his or her life that nothing the group does will get that person to consider the needs of the whole?

Does the person's behavior suggest strong feelings of not being acknowledged: "You're not listening to me, you're not giving me credit for how hard I'm trying in this group." Here, the person may not be playing power games or intending to be "difficult" but simply asking to be assured that you see him or her as a sincere and worthy member.

3. **Check the group as a whole:**

Is each person taking responsibility for co-facilitation by occasionally making observations on the process? Is it usually the same person who points out obvious discomfort in the group? When you comment, do you ask others whether they agree with your observation?

How would you characterize the group's response to the person whose comments or behavior seem to be causing problems? From the heart? Dispassionate? Analytical? Adversarial?

4. **Engage the person with a process comment:**

"I'm having a problem with something here. Would you please help me sort it out?"

> "I feel like I'm at a seminar that I didn't sign up for."
>
> "It feels as though we're taking positions on this subject and not letting ourselves go more deeply into unexamined territory."
>
> "It feels to me that we're spending too much time on one person's needs."
>
> "It seems like you're not here today, not present. What's going on for you?"
>
> (Notice that each of these comments begins with "I" or "it seems," not with an accusatory or a judging "You.")

Also, be prepared to experience what every practicing therapist knows: Insight is not equivalent to cure.

> *With my training as a therapist, I often have an idea about why a person or a group is stuck, yet I can't do much about it except point it out heartfully. Sometimes you can see how a person is stuck, but no amount of advice giving or well-timed input is going to help them out of their predicament. You can see how someone is hurting themselves but often you don't have any way of getting your awareness across so that it can be used. I'm not willing as a psychologist, or as a circle member, to pretend that I have any special tools that automatically help people get past a stuck place. I can think of an instance in which one woman who dominated a circle was clearly seen as the mother of the group, and everyone was deferential to her and accepted her ideas for discussion topics. It held the circle back from true co-facilitation. I mentioned that, but the group didn't have the willingness to work past it.*

5. **Offer the problem as "grist for the mill":**

Point out the problem behavior (again, in "I" terms, tell how it's affecting *you*), and then offer it to the group: "How do we all participate in this problem?"—after there's agreement that there is indeed a difficulty. You might get back some surprising answers: "I kind of like to hear John pontificate." "I feel so bad for Laurie and I didn't want to cut her off and seem as if I wasn't being compassionate." "I recognize that Justin is often coming from his head and not his heart, but I assumed he wasn't comfortable expressing his feelings." These responses may offer an opportunity to look more closely at the group's process and to learn what different behavioral norms have been assumed yet not explicitedly expressed.

6. **Make the circle the *dojo*, a place to practice listening:**

Listening to someone you like is usually easier than listening to someone who pushes your buttons, unless someone you like is presenting "tough stuff." The "practice" of listening may at times challenge you beyond your comfort zone. Listening to someone you have a hard time giving your heartful attention to may in fact force you to grow the most. In addressing some of the larger societal issues—ones that involve sexism, racism, poverty, and environmental assault—we are going to have to be able to engage people "from the heart" whose words and behaviors may be very difficult for us. Take the opportunity to stretch those heartstrings.

I have surprised myself when I just sit and let myself observe those differences that rub me the wrong way, when I'm making a judgment about a person having a kindergarten level of awareness, for instance. If I allow myself to be vulnerable and go past the resistance and judgment, an opening happens. It's humbling when you see an aspect of yourself in that other person. The differences may not get reconciled, but there's a deepening of connection and a healing that takes place. It's happened to me over and over again in circles—when I remember to stay open.

7. What's beyond the capacity of the group?

Participants in a wisdom circle are not expected to be therapists or professional crisis counselors. As we said earlier: A wisdom circle cannot do psychotherapy or any other mental health intervention any more than it can do bypass surgery. People with problems such as drug abuse, violent behavior, threats to commit suicide, chronic depression, psychotic episodes, or other serious psychological challenges need more help than a wisdom circle can offer. When it appears that someone in the group has a serious problem, approach him or her with the same sense of partnership and mutuality that you offer other members of the circle. Encourage that person to get the help she or he needs and, if possible, suggest an appropriate community agency or health professional. Such advice should be offered outside the circle unless the person has solicited suggestions from members in the circle.

Asking Someone to Leave

We all learn from diversity and the perspective that it brings. As in the rest of the natural world, monocultures tend toward weakness and isolation. At their best, our circles are tapestries where members bring their unique colors to the beauty and aliveness of the group.

However, sometimes the group has to acknowledge its limitations and inability to deal with a given individual. Asking someone to leave can be one of the most complicated and wrenching episodes that a circle can go through. Some groups negotiate the challenge well, while others choose to disband rather than hurt someone.

Here is what can happen if you ignore a difficult situation and simply let things go:

> *My men's group was basically dismantled by one individual who was going through a midlife crisis. The group ended up focusing all its attention on him week after week after week. He sucked up all the energy of the group until they became tired of it and decided not to call a meeting for the following week. That was the end.*

•

> *I was in a circle of women who met once a month. After a while I discovered I really disliked another woman. I talked about it outside the circle, but never to her, and the others kept encouraging me to say something in circle. After several years I finally got up the courage to say to her that I was very bothered by her consistent focus on material possessions. I exploded with all this pent-up emotion. Later, I was really sorry—not for what I said, but for the way I talked to her. My outburst was too much for the group to handle. It destroyed the circle. It ended within a month or two.*

Here are successful scenarios, times when groups have acknowledged and addressed their internal difficulties:

Two people both wanted to be in our circle, but they often felt chilly toward each other. I said to them at one point: "I'm feeling some tension between the two of you, and I think it's disrupting the group. Is there some way you can deal with it, either here or outside the circle?" They said they'd like the circle to witness their conversation, and they passed the stick. They were on their best behavior, speaking from the heart. (They were roommates and had issues about personal boundaries in their shared space.) The tension eased between them and for the group too. A couple of months later, one of them left of his own accord.

•

When our group has had a head-on collision between two people, the rest of us take turns trying to identify some aspect of the altercation with our own behavior. It might be the tendency to talk too much, or a stereotype we're holding about one or the other person or some piece of whatever the "presenting problem" is. When we are willing to tell the truth about ourselves, it's as if we're all involved in the altercation in some way. We believe that the two people are playing out some deeper division in the group as a whole and that we all need to look at the parts we're playing in it. This lets off steam in the situation and the issue becomes "our" problem rather than "their" problem. So far this has worked.

•

The Raven Lodge started when a lot of men said, "Hey, let's get together and drum. That's all I want to do."

Some men wanted to go deeper and discuss male-female relationships. They formed subgroups that became closed circles. Some of them came back to the Raven Lodge just to drum, but eventually they stopped coming. The Raven Lodge disbanded. It may be that it served its purpose.

•

We were forming a co-housing community and meeting in a circle open to anyone interested. We didn't apply any tests, the only criterion was wanting to be part of it. When a new family joined the circle, there was something off about the fit. More and more people started to feel disturbed, but nothing was said for a long time. Finally the couple who had invited them in the first place phoned the family and said it was clear that some of their stated needs weren't being met and that their goals were different from the rest of the group's. The new members were feeling the same way, so they dropped out. The situation was resolved fairly easily.

•

My women's group decided that after four years it was time to end the circle and move on. During the closing ceremony one woman took a ball of yarn she'd been using for crocheting and spontaneously threw it to another woman. As she did she spoke her gratitude to that woman for all she had learned from her. This woman threw the yarn to another and thanked her. This went on for some time until every woman had spoken to every other woman at least once. The yarn made a beautiful and colorful web, and we could each see how strongly we had been woven into each other's lives. We shed tears of sadness and tears of joy, knowing the connections between us would endure beyond the circle. The name of the group had been the Spider Lodge.

A circle is like any relationship that has a beginning and an end. Be mindful that when you agree to participate in a circle, you may have to leave at some point. Your life circumstances may change, or it may be that in circle some issue cannot be resolved, or at least addressed in a way everyone can accept. We have occasionally had people leave angry, which is hard on everyone—the person leaving and the rest of us. When a departure is disruptive, the circle needs to be rewoven.

What if you are the person being asked to leave? You have a number of options:

- **You could leave, as requested, without comment and perhaps lose an invaluable opportunity to express yourself and increase self-awareness.**
- **You could ask to stay, which would mean you are willing to examine your behavior seriously and invite others to do so as well.**
- **You could state your case, admitting that the request is very hurtful and asking the group to examine its motives. Perhaps you are being targeted as a scapegoat because of unspoken issues in the group. (See later section on Scapegoating.)**
- **Ask for help. Admit that your behavior is a problem, and ask someone in the group to be a mentor for you and model the changes the group is asking you to make.**

- **Consciously work on yourself in the circle. Make process comments about yourself during your turns with the talking stick. "I know I tend to go on and on with this kind of topic, so I'm monitoring myself. If someone else feels that I'm going on too long, please signal me."**

Taboos

The notion that all content is "fair game" in a wisdom circle is countered by the reality that *every* group has its taboo subjects. Acknowledging this is a healthy exercise. When a taboo subject is not identified, you may see avoidance behaviors. When the discussion turns in this direction, someone may try to change the subject, another may get angry, or an uncomfortable silence may settle like a pall over the group. Members may not understand their own discomfort.

A taboo may remain unstated until the members feel secure enough to talk about it. In Cindy's mother's group, the subject of abortion was taboo for nearly thirty years. By the 1980s, however, group members had shared so many births and deaths that they were capable of tackling most anything. Topics like abortion and homosexuality—and the changing popular opinion on these issues—could be openly discussed. Even more prickly than these, perhaps, for any circle is the issue of one member's sexual attraction for another. In a men's group composed of both homosexual and heterosexual members, one gay man's attraction for a straight man was obvious and finally commented upon. Later it became an open subject and a source of teasing and good humor for all concerned.

Is anger taboo in your group? Expressing anger is something that we may give lip service to: "Oh, of course, it's all right to get angry in our group." But often there is a strong, unexpressed norm prohibiting it. Why? An angry outburst may create anxiety in the rest of the group. It's useful to remember that anger is one of the few emotions powerful enough to ward off fear and allow us to vent hurt feelings. It gives us a surge of strength when we are feeling most vulnerable. Keeping our hearts open helps us to receive the anger and stay sensitive to the angry person's underlying feelings as well. Listening from the heart ultimately requires us to stand in the fire of someone else's pain and offer a compassionate presence. It takes self-discipline and much practice to hold onto a calm center in the midst of someone else's fury.

Wisdom circles involving social activists may discover that a member has an opinion contrary to the group's stated philosophy. Do such individuals get reprimanded and told there's "one right way" to think about such things? Does your environmental group care about the welfare of families of loggers who are chopping down old-growth forests? How does your pro-choice group respond to the abortion of a viable fetus? What attitude does your AIDS agency have toward people who practice unsafe sex and then cost taxpayers $100,000 each time they go into the hospital for an AIDS-related infection? Can we make allowances for kids who sell crack to feed themselves and their families? A wisdom circle is ideally a place where a "politically incorrect" idea can have a voice in the community.

Scapegoating

Every good family counselor or group therapist knows that small groups have a shadow side—those psychic dynamics that are not acknowledged because they have a negative character. Rather than addressing these shadow elements, we sometimes target an individual in the group as "the problem." That person often either is a victim of the misplaced anxieties of the group or obliges the group by playing out a tacitly designated role. A common example is the troubled adolescent who acts out the dysfunctionality of the family. In a circle, the person selected as a scapegoat could be the one who is chronically late, the one who is consistently trying to push the group out of its comfort zone, the one who talks too long, or the one who acts out the sexual undertone by flirting outrageously in the group. This person gets labeled as "the problem" when, in fact, he or she is acting out the group's wish to break its own unstated rules. The scapegoat functions to focus the group's energies on one "problem person" rather than deal with underlying group tensions. For instance, when Frank the "guru" pontificates, he allows the group to avoid engaging more personal, intimate material. The "problem family" in the housing co-op circle might have been the scapegoat for the group's own lack of clarity about its goals. It is surprising how easily a group can band together and "punish" one or more people rather than deal with its own shadow elements. Psychiatrist Arthur Colman defines scapegoating in this way:

> *The group is not to blame for its problems, its bad feelings, its pains, its defeats. These are the responsibility of a particular individual or subgroup—the scapegoat—who is perceived as being fundamentally different from the rest of the group and must be excluded or sacrificed in order for the group to survive and remain whole.*

Colman says that for any group to mature, it must identify its own tendency to place blame on a designated "other."

> *It follows that just as there is little individual development without facing the problem of one's shadow, there is little group development without facing the problem of the group's scapegoats. . . . Once the group no longer focuses on saviors, heroes, victims and enemies but on the contribution of each group member to the collective and the collective to each member, it enters a new level of development.*

Scapegoating is a complex process not easily discerned by people within the group, and it may even escape the eye of trained therapists. We raise it here as food for thought and suggest again that an important guideline for relating to someone's "problem behavior" is to try to see how the whole group is aiding and abetting it, that is, to explore how the group is using the problem person to avoid its own growth. In the world of substance abuse and recovery, the term "co-dependent" is used to identify a similar phenomenon. It's easy to blame an individual for his drinking or her addiction to heroin, but how are others helping to reinforce and perpetuate these behaviors? For instance, a wife may "need" her husband to be an alcoholic in order to not look at her own psychological problems. It's easier to point to him as the cause of all her misery. Part of your work in an ongoing group is to help everyone to realize what roles they may not be conscious of playing—how they may be enabling problem behavior in others—and consider how the group can function in a more conscious and healthy fashion.

Group dynamics expert Arnold Mindell also adds to our

understanding of the dark elements of group behavior and says we all must deal with our own "garbage":

> *Human groups are all characterized by the same garbage. Garbage becomes manifest in the secret thoughts we have about each other: Who earns what? Who is strongest? Who is weakest? Who is most intelligent or most beautiful? Who sleeps with whom? Who is an insider? Who is an outsider? Who has power? Who really determines what happens? Though fascinating, garbage is discarded because it opposes group ideologies, which usually have little humor about their shadows. . . . When the garbage is processed, it always creates greater connection and spirit between members. Yet most organizations are hopeless about ever bringing their garbage to light.*

Mindell humorously encourages those of us in groups to identify every so often what is hanging out in the garbage pail and process it as frequently as needed. An example of a helpful comment might be: "I'm getting the sense that whoever has the stick is making the rules up as we go." Or, "Do I detect some competition here between certain members regarding professional credentials?" As we all know, garbage that is attended to can become compost.

Co-facilitation Is Key

When tensions arise, we each need to assume our role as co-facilitator and actively engage the others. It is not just the "difficult people" but those who ignore them who can compromise a group and shorten its life. An uncomfortable situation can serve as a prime opportunity for enhancing its aliveness, for teaching members how to live the constants, and for developing a sense of humor about our human foibles. Undoubtedly it is easier to label someone a "difficult person" than it is to step forward and address the discord. Without such proactive effort, the circle cannot evolve. If your group doesn't experience a difficulty once in a while, it is safe to say it is languishing in a comfort zone and may be increasingly boring and dissatisfying to its members.

What we are emphasizing is not "how to cope with difficult people" but how the group can benefit from the inevitable rough edges. What holds people in the circle? What makes people value a circle? How is it that some people will stick through all the problems we've mentioned and still hang in there? It turns out that how we handle the interpersonal dynamics is a primary reason for meeting in the first place. A sense of community, a desire for self-exploration, and a hunger for the strength of kindred spirits is what motivates many of us to persevere in circles. Feeling safe enough to present yourself authentically with your hard-won insights, along with all your vulnerabilities, is such a rare experience for most of us that it is worth traversing the rough but fertile ground we find along the way.

The mountain does not laugh at the river because it is lowly, nor does the river speak ill of the mountain because it cannot move about.

—Japanese proverb

SIXTEEN

Ceremonial Circles

When we are aware of our place in the larger scheme of things, daily life becomes more spontaneous and meaningful, and our actions serve life naturally. We are called beyond an introverted spirituality to consider everything in our dealings with others as part of our spiritual life.

—*Elizabeth Roberts,* Life Prayers

~

What image do the words "spring ritual" conjure up for you? How about "harvest festival"? Do you mark the winter and summer solstices as they pass? Even though most of us are far removed from the seasonal ceremonies that used to dot the lives of our ancestors for thousands of years, we can still appreciate the social cohesion and stability provided by those events. The turning of the seasons and the great religious festivals all call for ceremony—they are opportunities for us to renew our relationship to the

Source of Life and to the rhythms of nature. They connect us to the great round of creation, the universal pattern of birth, growth, fullness, death, and decay. As Elizabeth Roberts says in *Earth Prayers*: "Our psychic energies are renewed in their deepest sources by participation in the cycles of change in the natural world."

A Time and Place to Renew

Wisdom circles lend themselves to ceremonies that mark the seasons—to winter solstice events such as Hanukkah, Christmas, and Kwanzaa, to the coming of spring and events such as Easter and Passover, to the holidays of summer and to the introspective holy days of the fall, including Yom Kippur and All Hallow's Eve. Wisdom circles can also be called to celebrate individual milestones, including births, birthdays, graduations, and anniversaries. They are a fine way to mark both beginnings and endings, from an announcement of a marital engagement to a memorial to honor the life of someone who has died. A wisdom circle can bring aliveness and new meaning to occasions that have become habitual or routine. It can also honor rites of passage and other life events that our culture doesn't often recognize ceremonially, such as the onset of puberty, menopause, the loss of a pet, the trauma of physical violence, or the end of a relationship. Holding a circle to express gratitude for blessings received is also a nice way to spend that time between dinner and dessert on Thanksgiving Day.

When Charlie and Cindy moved into their home in Oakland in 1988, they held a large housewarming circle. Each person was asked to speak to what "home" meant to them and offer a blessing for the house. When Cindy turned fifty, Charlie put together a wisdom circle for her and designed special T-shirts for each attendee. As ritual objects, he provided a highly decorated bottle of red wine and the blue and white ceramic goblet used at his and Cindy's wedding. Everyone in the circle took a turn pouring a little wine into the goblet and then spoke to Cindy about their friendship. One friend recalled their days together when Cindy was a radio newscaster. Another wrote a poem that ended with "One-of-a-kind woman, one-of-a-kind celebration." After the last person spoke, Cindy took the goblet filled to the brim with loving thoughts and drank from it.

A Wedding Circle

We recently participated in a wedding that used the wisdom circle format and opened with the following invocation:

Great Mystery, Great Spirit, That which makes sacred every leaf and every drop of water. Great Earth which holds a bountiful community of beings, the Source of Life. We gather in a circle today to create a sacred container for love to flourish. We join with the Earth and with each other to surround Linda and John with our love, with our support and with our gratitude for their commitment to each other.

Linda and John give the gift of reminding us how much stronger and how much more radiant we are when we join our soul with that of another. As they speak of their love and commitment, let us renew our commitments to ourselves, to all those we love, and to the sacred flowering Earth.

We ask the Spirit of Joy to enter our circle, to lift up our hearts, and to help us remember that when two people express love for one another, all creation rejoices. We ask the Spirit of Plenty to enter our circle to bless both Linda and John with an abundance of the gifts of the material world. We ask the Spirit of Beauty to fill their lives with the delicious pleasures of the senses, and the Spirit of Health to support them in long and active lives. We ask the Spirit of Love that brought them together at Martha's Coffee House to continue to guide their steps on the journey to deeper and deeper relationship. We ask that same Spirit of Love to reside in their hearts forever. May John and Linda walk together in Joy, in Plenty, in Beauty, in Health, and in Love.

After the invocation, each person in attendance gave the couple a rose. This became part of a beautiful bouquet for them to hold as they spoke their marriage vows.

A Healing Circle

When a circle member gets hit hard by life through a serious diagnosis or major loss, a healing circle can be very supportive. In traditional societies, the community forms a supportive net holding the patient and the healer. Healing ourselves involves restoring the health of the spirit while repairing the connections between body and mind, self and other, self and nature. Healing can occur in a circle when the wounded person has the opportunity to talk about the pain, to grieve the loss. One woman used the circle to express her difficulty in moving from a much beloved place:

> *One of our members was in the process of moving out of her home of many years. She brought a big packing box into the middle of the circle and climbed inside. Soon garments, books, and other things began flying out of*

the box. Most of us in the circle chuckled until suddenly there was a wrenching sound. Inside the box she was ripping a piece of fabric to pieces, showing us how her heart was being torn apart by this uprooting of her life. I learned more about this woman and her pain in this wordless demonstration than I could have ever known through words.

•

Ramsy, my cat, died of kidney failure when he was twelve years old. I loved him very much. He touched a part of me that I let few people see. After we buried him in the backyard, I held a memorial circle with three other people who knew him well. I brought out all the wonderful pictures I took of him over the years and we told "Ramsy stories." I had the chance to say what I learned from this gentle teacher and have the others bear witness.

Other kinds of painful separations can be witnessed in a wisdom circle. A couple who was separating called a circle of people who had witnessed their wedding:

The couple understood that the parting would have an impact on their friends and on the community. They didn't want anyone to take sides. They also wanted to stay friends and have the circle witness that commitment. The circle was formed with drumming and singing, and the four directions were called in. The couple sat in the center, and a friend tied their wrists together with yarn. As the talking stick was passed, the group reflected on their personal relationships with each of them and how much they appreciated them. The cou-

ple then explained why the time had come to end their marriage. At the closing of the circle, the friend who had tied the wrists together took a knife and cut the cord.

A wisdom circle can be a safe place to find or offer forgiveness, to acknowledge an injustice that one has suffered or committed, or to let go of old emotional baggage full of resentment or blame. On the one-year anniversary of their circle, five men held a ceremony to honor their experience at the front lines of the AIDS epidemic. They each lit a candle and spoke about the ways they kept their hearts open while witnessing the suffering of so many friends and the deaths of so many people at an early age.

The person who is the focus of a healing circle can sit in the middle if she is comfortable doing so. The hurting person is often not able to design a ritual, so it's up to other members to plan it. In a healing circle, it is especially important to keep the ritual simple; each person should have the opportunity to speak. Keep in mind as you plan the ceremony that it is not a performance intended to impress an audience. Rather, it is a communication with the divine wisdom of healing that is within each one of us.

I tripped at a dance and broke a bone in my foot, which was taking months to heal. I hobbled in on crutches into my women's circle and asked if we could take some time to make it a healing circle for me. The women gathered around me, each placing a hand on my foot cast. Everyone spoke her wish for the bone to heal; then we sat in silence for several minutes, imagining that we were creating a pool of healing energy for me to draw upon.

The love and support I felt that afternoon certainly made a difference. Within a week, I felt the bone was greatly improved.

The primary purpose in a healing circle is to allow a person to give voice to the pain or loss and then reconnect to the larger community. Even though we know that life contains illness and tragedy for everyone, when they occur, that plaintive voice still cries, "Why me?" The circle can help us remember that in these extraordinary moments we are not alone.

Several years ago, I [Sedonia] was involved in a healing circle of more than two hundred people. A teenage girl from my community was killed in a senseless and very tragic way, and we wanted to honor her as well as comfort the grieving parents. Our community met frequently in a dozen overlapping circles, and because of those years of experience, this circle held much power. It felt as if we had entered a deep well together, where we could safely feel all our emotions, and then were able to spiral up to find healing and strength and offer it to the parents. It was a very moving and beautiful circle as people of all ages and backgrounds bonded together in love and grief. There was time for anyone who wished to speak. A very broad range of emotions was expressed, from anger over the unfairness of this death, to laughter, as we shared anecdotes about the slain girl.

This particular circle touched our community in many precious ways. In the months that followed, we held a regular women's circle to support the mother, and each woman expressed how especially dear her family had become to her through this grieving process. They also expressed their fears for their own safety and for their daughters and later went through a self-defense training course. The men held a healing circle for the father in a sweat lodge setting. The teenagers in the community met in ongoing circles to express their feelings and fears. Because the man who murdered the teenager was of another race, we arranged for antiracist training for the teenagers. Everyone who went through this process desired to make more time for their families.

This circle was particularly meaningful to me because my mother died quite suddenly when I was fourteen months old. She was twenty-two, and I was raised by her parents. Their grief permeated the household. Watching Karen go through her grief allowed me to see deeply into it. It has healed something in me because it helped me understand the context I was raised in. I now understand my grandmother in ways that I never could before. This event, perhaps more than any other I've participated in, helped me remember why we circle—so we can be ready to touch the meaning and the mystery in those very big events that shape our lives. We circle so we can create the kind of supportive community that we all need and want.

Masks and Shields

You can add another dimension of creativity and fun to your circle, especially those that honor the seasons and joyous rites of passage, with the use of masks. They can be a useful tool to invoke a more spontaneous self. Masks give us permission to suspend our usual personas and to encourage other aspects of our personalities to show up. One night the Daughters of Eos decorated each other's faces as goddesses, using theatrical paints and cosmetics. A group of women going through menopause made masks of themselves as crones. They wore them in the circle, and they talked about how they would like to be in their old age. In a ceremonial circle designed by Buddhist philosopher Joanna Macy and ecologist John Seed, participants make animal masks and then present what they believe to be the concerns of their chosen animal. This circle is called "The Council of All Beings."

A mask can be composed simply of theatrical face paint or purchased in toto in a store. Also, easy instruction books on how to make papier mâché masks can be found in the children's section of many bookstores.

Creating a group shield is also fun and provides a visual symbol for the circle. Shields have a long history of representing families and groups. Some European families have coats of arms that go back hundreds of years. Native American tribes also create shields to honor their power animals and other elements of nature. Creating a shield can be a bonding exercise, the completed shield standing as a physical reminder of the commitment of the group. In Sedonia's Owl/Eagle Lodge, an artistic member drew an owl and an eagle with overlapping wings on a piece of leather stretched onto a hoop. Each member tied a feather to the bottom of the hoop, declaring what she brought to the group, what she needed from it, and her level of commitment. When someone leaves the lodge, another ceremony is held in which each member removes her feather and ties a small shadow feather in its place so that the shield holds a reminder of her presence in the group.

How to Plan a Ceremony

Often one member of a circle feels the need to have an important event honored with ceremony and asks the group to help create it. A ceremonial circle can take up the entire time of the gathering or be scheduled at the beginning or end of a regular meeting. There are many ways to create a ritual honoring an event. A number of books on ritual are available in most bookstores.

Even if one person is taking responsibility for organizing the ceremony, be sure that each member plays a part. There is no right or wrong way to create a ceremony, but simplicity is often better than an elaborate or complex activity. As you plan your ceremony, ask the following questions:

What is the intention of the ceremony?

What symbolic objects best capture that intention?

Will one person lead the whole ceremony or simply initiate each round?

Shall we compose a special prayer or invocation for this occasion?

How will we end the ceremony in a clear way that allows a sense of completion?

It is an art to encourage full participation and make the ceremony meaningful for everyone. The most successful ceremonies acknowledge our major transition points and our connection to each other. At the heart of every ceremony is the desire to honor the Web of Life.

This lovely Buddhist invocation is appropriate for many ceremonial occasions:

May I be filled with lovingkindness, may I be well.
May I be peaceful and at ease, may I be happy.

May you be filled with lovingkindness, may you be well.
May you be peaceful and at ease, may you be happy.

May we be filled with lovingkindness, may we be well.
May we be peaceful and at ease, may we be happy.

SEVENTEEN

The Circle of Life

In this final chapter we want to fit wisdom circles into a larger context and share our vision for their potential. Let's examine how circles can strengthen our lives and serve as yeast for our world.

It's time to go beyond talking about the changes we would like to make in ourselves, our relationships, and our communities. It's time to go beyond hoping that we can end the violence of human against human, wishing that we could halt the degradation of the environment and the destruction of our fellow creatures. It's time to recognize that giving lip service and a donation or two to the causes we care about will not make an appreciable difference.

Talking, hoping, and visioning are all requisite phases in the process of creation. But only conscious action informed by a vision of a world that works for everyone will effect healthy change. Creation is a fundamental aspect of life, and our most important creation is ourselves in service to our highest values. It is time to call forth the qualities of life we want to live: Love, Compassion, Courage, Truth, Generosity, Joy, Laughter, Peace, Respect, Beauty, Harmony. We invoke their presence to root them more deeply in our lives right now. We are reminded of the couplet by Goethe: "Whatever you can do, or dream you can, begin it. Boldness has genius, power and magic in it." Begin a wisdom circle. Better yet, let's live the wisdom circle constants together.

Our Vision for Wisdom Circles

We see the circle as part of a spiritual movement. Its principal value is the spirit of inquiry—something that hasn't always been valued in spiritual movements of the past. It is a spirit of inquiry that eschews dogmatism and honors "many paths." This movement uses ritual and symbols that are meaningful to us now, not those that have long since lost their meaning and their power to inspire us.

The other central value of wisdom circles is compassion. The importance of compassion is emphasized at the beginning of most spiritual movements; then later in their development the "one and only way to be spiritual" takes hold, and compassion is reserved for "our own" but not for other people. The compassion of wisdom circles extends to everyone; it also includes reverence for the Earth and for the environment we share. Wisdom circles are part of a larger consciousness pressing to be born; it is a form we can all use to express a free, unbiased spirit of inquiry and heartfelt compassion and bring them into daily life.

The wisdom circle is also a place where we can begin to claim our inner authority. As we learn to trust ourselves, we start to understand that each one of us has a contribution to make to the whole and to the problems we are collectively facing. We begin to realize that no one else is going to solve these problems for us. The answers are not going to come from experts, but from everybody, with even the smallest voices heard and acknowledged with heart. The circle is a place to practice giving voice to that inner authority as an antidote to relinquishing our power and complying with the beliefs and agendas of others. We can also examine old assumptions and discard them when a deeper truth presents itself.

Viable to the Self and Workable in the World

Many of the people we know who sit in circle consider it part of their spiritual practice. A wisdom circle can be a tool like meditation, a way of accessing the spiritual without an intermediary. It is a practice that many people know about and which some use regularly and some on occasion. The constants provide a common language we can use to talk to each other about our values and visions.

The circle is becoming a tool for transformation not only at the personal level but at the archetypal level. The archetype of the rugged individualist at the core of Western conquest and civilization appears now to be taking a back seat to the archetype of the fully participating partner, a member of the Round Table—an archetype realizing itself in the consciousness of women and men who recognize that service to the whole is what survival of the species depends on. We are being asked—by our nature and by Nature itself—to rediscover ourselves, as humans, as members of a tribe or collective. Circles challenge us to move past our isolated self-concerns—from seeing ourselves as separate, too often doing whatever we want no matter what the consequences, to seeing ourselves as connected, participating in a multicultural global community.

The circle is a spiritual practice with very practical application in the world. Many hundreds of circles are composed of people who gather together in each other's homes to facilitate self-discovery and build compassionate community, and these circles give them support in handling the rest of their lives. We also see wisdom circles working well in health-care organizations, in the nonprofit sector, in government and corporate settings—wherever there is a need to allow the hard-earned wisdom of individual members to surface in order to improve the functioning of the whole. Employees are often viewed by their leaders as if they are cogs in a large machine. Many organizations that are run essentially as machines need a new infusion of life, a new sense of mission, a new understanding of the people in them. The wisdom circle can be the "heartspace" that helps institutions function productively and in a more humane way.

A wisdom circle has the potential to heal separations in many settings. We feel a bonding with the people in our circles and then find ourselves taking that increased potential for relationship out into the world. The deep, warm, strong connections in circle become the standard for our relationships everywhere. Rather than the circle being an exceptional situation, it is a natural meeting ground. The circle is a *dojo*—a practice arena—for an opening of the heart. We invite you to join us and explore this process for yourself in the company of kindred spirits.

Let's close our circle with a meditation on a quote from philosopher Huston Smith:

Infinite gratitude toward all things past

Infinite service toward all things present

Infinite responsibility toward all things future

Summary of the Ten Constants

Constant One: *Honor the circle as sacred time and space* by doing simple rituals to mark the circle's opening and closing. Light candles, or take a few moments to breathe deeply and meditate. Burn some incense or sage. Listen to a selection of evocative music or a guided meditation. You can be as creative as you want with these rituals.

Constant Two: *Create a collective center.* Make a physical center in the room. Mutually agree upon a topic or question that will serve as the central focus. A group may choose an issue specific to its needs, or it can allow for topics to surface determined by individual members' needs.

Constant Three: *Ask to be informed* by our highest human values such as compassion and truth, by the wisdom of those who have gone before us, and by the needs of those yet to be born. You can also invoke mythical or historical figures who symbolize desired values. One person can speak for the group, or each member can do a personal invocation.

Constant Four: *Express gratitude* for the blessings and teachings of life. Acknowledge and honor our interdependence with everything in the Web of Life. In silence, or by taking turns, give thanks for those people and those things great and small whose gifts enrich and nourish you.

Constant Five: *Create a safe container for full participation and deep truth-telling.* Allow each person to speak without interruption or cross-talk. Pass the talking stick (or any object that has symbolic significance) around the circle, until everyone has the opportunity to participate. Respect a member's right to silence. Keep everything confidential.

Constant Six: *Listen from the heart,* and serve as compassionate witness for the other people in the circle. To be an effective witness, pay attention to what's being said without interrupting, judging, or trying to "fix" or rescue the person speaking. Be willing to discover something about yourself in the stories of other people.

Constant Seven: *Speak from the heart and from direct experience.* When you are moved to speak, do so thoughtfully and with care. Avoid abstract, conceptual language, and stay in touch with your feelings as much as possible. As this capacity develops, you may be moved to share your deepest feelings and to say difficult things without self-judgment and without blaming others.

Constant Eight: *Make room for silence to enter.* During the circle, allow for reflection and meditation and for deep feelings to surface. Silence enhances *temenos* as the group proceeds.

Constant Nine: *Empower each member to be a co–facilitator of the process.* If possible, designate a different person to be the circle maker each time. This person readies the physical setting, initiates the opening and closing rituals, and facilitates consensus on a topic. Encourage each other to give voice to feelings of satisfaction or discomfort about the group's process.

Constant Ten: *Commit to an ongoing relationship* with the people in your circle to engender trust and caring among them. Extend that caring to other people, to the Earth and all its creatures by practicing the capacities developed within the wisdom circle in daily life.

A Wisdom Circle

The following is a meditation that brings together the opening invocations of Chapters 1–10. Reading it aloud can serve as an opening ritual for your group. It touches on all the intentions of the wisdom circle.

Meditation

Welcome to the circle. Let us proceed to clear a place for Spirit to enter, and take a moment to feel our soul connections. Close your eyes and notice your breathing. Allow your breath to carry you deeper and deeper into yourself, far, far back into time—into a time when your ancestors met in circles. Perhaps you can hear the drums, feel the warmth of the tribal fire on your face, feel the bonds of kinship and belonging. Each and every one of us has ancestors who sat around a fire together, drumming, singing, dancing, telling stories, praying to the spirit of the sacred place on Earth that they knew as home. In those circles people spoke from the heart, they found solutions to their problems, they laughed and they played, they celebrated and they grieved together. The memory of this time is in your body, in your bones, in your belly. It is your deep connection to the circle. It is your heritage. The time has come to remember the circle and bring this way of gathering back into our consciousness, into our lives and into community.

We gather around the flame of wisdom's light and warmth to discover what gifts we have brought with us and what we have learned from our time on Earth—that delicate blend of embracing the Source of Life and the Web of Life. This circle marks the center of the world, our world in this moment. Let this center focus our hearts and minds and connect us to each other and shift our consciousness from our individual existence to the larger Web of Life. It is here we begin to know ourselves as members of a group and begin to feel the group within ourselves.

We call on our highest selves, on Love, Compassion, Courage, Truth, Generosity, Joy, Laughter, Peace, Respect, Beauty, and Harmony. We ask that these qualities that dwell within each of us be conscious and present for us all.

We are grateful for this gathering, which offers us nourishment for our souls and brings wisdom to our lives. We feel deep gratitude to the Earth, our home, for sustaining us and teaching us how to live in harmony with all our fellow creatures. We thank each individual who has come today to listen and to speak from the heart. Let's acknowledge the joy and strength we receive from this communion.

[PAUSE]

This circle is a home where we feel known, trusted, and valued. It is a safe container where we can draw upon our innate capacities for wisdom, compassion, and self-healing. We humans have depended on such capacities for millennia. We have also depended on each other for a sense of sanctuary. In this circle, each of us can reveal our fears, show our vulnerabilities, and give voice to our dreams. This is a safe space where we can begin a "foolish project" like learning to live together in harmony. It's time to begin such a "foolish project."

Let us remember that the talking stick or stone serves the listeners as much as it does the speaker. It teaches us how to listen—respectfully, with full attention. It asks us to quiet the internal voice, the one that tends to evaluate, compare, disagree, and judge. It reminds us that we are each trying to speak from the heart as best we can. At any moment, something may be said that is exactly what we need to hear—and it may surprise us.

Come to the wisdom circle with this hope in your heart:

> *Let me see the world through your eyes, hear the world as you hear it. Let us teach each other, support each other, inspire each other, and heal each other. Let us make visible to ourselves, and then to the world, how much we care.*

It is time to listen deeply to that "still small voice within" and let its message coalesce into a soul-force. This circle is a sacred place where we find our authentic voice—the one that contributes to the wisdom of the whole. Finding our own courage and strength, knowing that they are alive and well within each of us, will make it possible for others to find those qualities within themselves. May every person in this circle become the seed for a hundred new ideas and for ten creative solutions to each problem we face.

Let us also make room for silence to enter our wisdom circle. As we sit in silence together, we can let deeper intuitions surface. This is the time to clear our minds. This is the time for whatever has been hanging back in the recesses of our consciousness to show up and be heard.

Let us be companions in the quest that never ceases—the inquiry into who we are and why we are here. We remind each other of our inner truths and support each other in living our beauty. What a rare experience!—to feel equally empowered to hold the circle, to question the process, to be held as vital and sacred by the others.

Within this community are gifts for healing the world, for learning to live in harmony with one another and with the Earth. We call upon ourselves to witness our commitment to the circle, and to our own personal development. The more we commit to the highest values held by this group, the more we are empowered to give voice to those values. We are present here to discover our own wisdom and compassion and to bear witness to the wisdom and compassion that dwell within the hearts of each of us. May it be so.

Notes

page 1: The John Seed quote appears in *Earth Prayers from Around the World, 365 Prayers, Poems and Invocations for Honoring the Earth*, edited by Elizabeth Roberts and Elias Amidon (HarperSanFrancisco, 1991), p. 35.

Introduction

page 7: For further details and an analysis of the Gallup Foundation poll, see *Sharing the Journey, Support Groups and America's New Quest for Community*, by Robert Wuthnow (The Free Press, 1994).

page 7: Paul Ray's quote is from a prepublication manuscript, used with permission of the author. For more on his study, see *Integral Culture Survey*, research paper 96A, 1996, published by the Institute of Noetic Sciences (475 Gate Five Rd., Sausalito, CA 94965).

Chapter 1

page 21: *Rilke's Book of Hours*, translated by Anita Barrows and Joanna Macy (Riverhead, 1996), p. 48.

page 22: For a further discussion of ancient conceptions of sacred time and space, see *The Myth of the Eternal Return*, by Mircea Eliade (Princeton University Press; latest printing, 1991).

page 23: Living in the present moment is a recurring theme in all of Thich Nhat Hanh's works. We recommend his *Understanding Peace* (Parallax Press, 1987).

page 24: The reference to the Sumerian circle is found in *The Power of Myth,* by Joseph Campbell with Bill Moyers (Doubleday, 1988), p. 215.

page 28: The cat story is found in *Soul Food: Stories to Nourish the Spirit and the Heart*, edited by Christina Feldman and Jack Kornfield (HarperSanFrancisco, 1991), p. 249.

page 30: *The Eternal Now*, by Paul Tillich (Scribner's, 1963), p. 168.

Chapter 2

page 31: *He: Understanding Masculine Psychology*, by Robert A. Johnson (Harper and Row, 1989), p. 82.

page 36: James Hillman's quote is found in his introduction to *Ecopsychology: Restoring the Earth, Healing the Mind*, edited by Theodore Roszak, Mary E. Gomes, and Allen Kanner (Sierra Club Books, 1995), p. xviii.

page 36: John Seed's quote is found in *World as Lover, World as Self*, by Joanna Macy (Parallax Press, 1991), p. 184.

page 38: All of Arthur Colman's quotes are taken from his book *Up from Scapegoating, Awakening Consciousness in Groups* (Chiron Publications, 1995). This quote is found on p. 52.

page 42: Fran Peavey's essay on "Strategic Questioning" can be found in *Insight and Action: How to Discover and Support a Life of Integrity and Commitment to Change*, by Tova Green and Peter Woodrow (New Society Publishers, 1994). This book also contains useful circle questions for activists.

Chapter 3

page 48: The Chinook invocation appears in Roberts and Amidon, *Earth Prayers*, p. 107.

page 50: See *Living Buddha, Living Christ*, by Thich Nhat Hanh (Riverhead Books, 1995).

page 51: *Desert Wisdom, Sacred Middle Eastern Writings from the Goddess through the Sufis*, translation and commentary by Neil Douglas-Klotz (HarperSanFrancisco, 1995), p. 193.

page 55: See *The Ceremonial Circle* by Sedonia Cahill and Joshua Halpern (HarperSanFrancisco, 1991), for further information on earth-centered spirituality.

Chapter 4

page 58: These AIDS caregiver stories and others can be found in *Sometimes My Heart Goes Numb, Love and Caregiving in a Time of AIDS*, by Charles Garfield with Cindy Spring and Doris Ober (Jossey-Bass Publishers, 1995).

page 61: Elizabeth Roberts's quote is found in Roberts and Amidon, *Earth Prayers*, p. 211.
page 65: *Being Home, A Book of Meditations*, by Gunilla Norris (Bell Tower, 1991), p. 4.

Chapter 5

page 66: James Baldwin's quote is found in *Loneliness and Love*, by Clark E. Moustakas (Prentice-Hall, 1972), p. 126.
page 78: *The Way of Council*, by Jack Zimmerman with Virginia Coyle (Bramble Books, 1996).

Chapter 6

page 81: *Kitchen Table Wisdom, Stories That Heal*, by Rachel Naomi Remen, M.D. (Riverhead Books, 1996), p. 149.
page 84: Carl Rogers, "Empathic: An Unappreciated Way of Being," in *The Counseling Psychologist*, Vol. 5 (1975), p. 4.
page 84: For further information on the Greenblatt study, see *The Broken Heart, The Medical Consequences of Loneliness*, by James J. Lynch (BasicBooks, 1977), p. 97.
page 87: The Virginia Satir comment is from a personal conversation with Cindy Spring.
page 90: Arnold Mindell's quote is taken from his interview, *Worldwork*, appearing in *New Dimensions, The Journal of New Dimensions Radio*, Vol. 23, No. 2 (April–June 1996), p. 13.
page 92: Macy, *World as Lover*, p. 183.
page 92: Colman, *Up from Scapegoating*, p. 49.
page 93: Colman, ibid., p. 60.

Chapter 7

page 95: *The Heart Aroused, Poetry and the Preservation of the Soul in Corporate America*, by David Whyte (Currency/Doubleday, 1994), p. 120.
page 97: *The Inner Story*, by Helen Luke (Crossroad, 1982), p. 5.
page 97: Whyte, *Heart Aroused*, p. 120.
page 100: *Sacred Path Cards*, by Jamie Sams (HarperSan Francisco, 1990), p. 275.

page 101: *Out of Solitude*, by Henri Nouwen (Ave Maria Press, 1974), p. 35.

page 102: Many useful questions for wisdom circles can be found in *The Four-Fold Way, Walking the Paths of the Warrior, Teacher, Healer and Visionary*, by Angeles Arrien (HarperSan Francisco, 1993).

page 107: Remen, *Kitchen Table Wisdom*, p. xxvi.

page 110: *The Color of Fear* is a provocative documentary film that can be used in discussions about racism. Information and video copies can be obtained from Stir Fry Seminars, 470 Third Street, Oakland, CA 94607, (510) 419-3930.

Chapter 8

page 113: *The Bow and the Lyre*, by Octavio Paz (University of Texas Press, 1973), p. 131.

page 115: *Focusing*, by Eugene T. Gendlin (Bantam, 1981), p. 90.

page 116: For an in-depth understanding of Nouwen's comment, see *With Open Hands* (Ave Maria Press, 1976), pp. 25–88.

page 119: *Sharing Silence, Meditation Practice and Mindful Living*, by Gunilla Norris (Bell Tower, 1992), p. 13.

Chapter 9

page 122: *The Year I, Global Process Work*, by Arnold Mindell (Arkana, 1989), p. 89. Used with permission of author.

page 126: Macy, *World as Lover*, p. 30.

Chapter 10

page 134: This quote from philosopher and social theorist Lewis Mumford can be found in "The Last Days of Lewis Mumford," by Tonia Shoumatoff in *Lapis* magazine, No. 3 (1996), p. 61.

Chapter 11

page 165: Lynne Twist's quote is from her interview, *The Soul of Money*, appearing in *New Dimensions, The Journal of New Dimensions Radio*, Vol. 24, No. 1 (Jan.–Feb. 1997), p. 23.

page 167: *Calling the Circle: The First and Future Culture*, by Christina Baldwin (Swan Raven and Company, 1994), p. 11.

page 168: Hollye Hurst's quote is from her article "Ritual Revival and the Circle of Community," appearing in *Creation Spirituality* magazine (Winter 1995), p. 47.

page 169: *Life Prayers from Around the World, 365 Prayers, Blessings, and Affirmations to Celebrate the Human Journey*, edited by Elizabeth Roberts and Elias Amidon (Harper SanFrancisco, 1996).

page 170: See Suggested Resources section for more information on *The Warrior.*

page 170: *Images and Symbols, Studies in Religious Symbolism*, by Mircea Eliade (Princeton University Press, 1991), p. 54.

page 173: Gratitude to Larry Yang for the use of his closing invocation.

Chapter 13

page 175: For a fuller analysis of Parsifal and the Grail story, see Johnson, *He.*

page 180: Barbara Sher's question comes from her book *Live the Life You Love* (Bantam, 1996).

page 186: *Letters to a Young Poet*, by Rainer Maria Rilke (W. W. Norton, 1934), p. 35.

Chapter 15

page 201: For additional discussion of contemporary Mahayana Buddhism, see Macy, *World as Lover*, and *The Illustrated World's Religions*, by Huston Smith (HarperSanFrancisco, 1994).

page 216: For a fuller discussion of how to handle the scapegoat role in a group, see *The Leader as Martial Artist*, by Arnold Mindell (HarperSanFrancisco, 1992), p. 59.

page 219: Colman, *Up from Scapegoating*, p. 81.

page 220: Colman, ibid., p. 81.

page 221: Mindell, *The Year I*, p. 94. Used with permission of author.

Chapter 16

page 223: Roberts and Amidon, *Life Prayers*, p. xix.

page 224: Roberts and Amidon, *Earth Prayers*, p. 283.

page 231: A complete version of The Council of All Beings process is found in *Thinking Like a Mountain, Towards a Council of All Beings*, by John Seed, Joanna Macy, Pat Fleming, and Arne Naess (New Society Publishers, 1988).

Chapter 17

page 238: The Huston Smith quote was taken from *The Wisdom of Faith*, a video series by Bill Moyers with Huston Smith. Used with permission of the author.

We are also grateful for the inspiration and insight we obtained from:

The Politics of Meaning, Restoring Hope and Possibility in an Age of Cynicism, by Michael Lerner (Addison-Wesley, 1996).

The Re-Enchantment of Everyday Life, by Thomas Moore (HarperCollins, 1996).

The Little Book of Big Questions, 200 Ways to Explore Your Spiritual Nature, by Jonathan Robinson (Conari Press, 1995).

Suggested Resources

Books

Sedonia Cahill and Joshua Halpern, *The Ceremonial Circle: Practice, Ritual and Renewal for Personal and Community Healing*. HarperSanFrancisco, 1990.

Christina Baldwin, *Calling the Circle: The First and Future Culture*. Swan Raven and Company, 1994.

Bill Kauth, *A Circle of Men: The Original Manual for Men's Support Groups*. New York: St. Martin's Press, 1992.

Jack Zimmerman with Virginia Coyle, *The Way of Council.* Bramble Books, 1996.

Organizations

The Institute of Noetic Sciences (IONS) offers leading-edge research in consciousness. Some IONS chapters in the United States conduct wisdom circles as an activity for members. They can be reached at 475 Gate Five Rd. #300, Sausalito, CA 94965, (415) 331-5650.

New Dimensions Radio through its broadcasts on NPR stations and its large selection of audio tapes offers a diversity of views from many traditions and cultures to help foster healthy personal and planetary development. Their quarterly journal contains information on participating in the Earth Circle prayer/meditation that takes place on the first day of each month at the same time around the globe. A chart gives you the time for your location. They can be reached at P.O. Box 569, Ukiah, CA 95482.

Compact disks available from Wisdom Circles

The Ceremonial Circle: Invoking an Earth-Centered Wisdom Circle, with Sedonia Cahill. Ten tracks of spoken word with music, drumming, and invocations. Length: 60 minutes.

The Warrior: Living the Four-Fold Way, with Angeles Arrien. Ten tracks of spoken word with music and invocations. Length: 60 minutes.

The Healer: Living the Four-Fold Way, with Angeles Arrien. Nine tracks of spoken word with music including a healing journey. Length: 55 minutes.

Listening from the Heart, Building Compassionate Community, with Charles Garfield and Cindy Spring. Ten tracks of spoken word with music including exercises for the practice of active listening. Length: 60 minutes.

For more information on the wisdom circles network and on the compact discs, please contact Wisdom Circles by mail at 3756 Grand Ave. #405, Oakland, CA 94610, or by phone at (510) 272-9540. Our e-mail address is: wisdomcircle@igc.apc.org

Acknowledgments

We are most indebted to our ancestors who sat around those campfires long ago whose courage to persevere helped bring us to this point in history. We honor you for the legacy of life-affirming wisdom you have given us. We extend our admiration to those people throughout the United States and abroad who called circles well before any of us were involved.

Our deepest gratitude goes to Valerie Andrews for her skilled writing and editorial work. Her expertise and commitment have made this book much more readable. Above and beyond her ability to slash redundancies and create important transitions, Valerie brought keen insight to the topics themselves that added richness to our ideas.

Special thanks go to the members of the Wisdom Circles Advisory Circle who continue to help us vision our future as well as offer support to the increasing number of wisdom circles worldwide: Tom Hurley of the Institute of Noetic Sciences, Michael Toms and Justine Toms of New Dimensions Radio, Joseph Tieger of the *Reaching Out* video series, Alexandra Hart, editor of *Perspective*, the Association for Humanistic Psychology newsletter, and Gayle Waring, minister of the United Church of Christ in Cloverdale, California. Thanks also to everyone at IONS and New Dimensions for their continued support.

For help with the material in Chapter 15, we owe a debt of gratitude to a group of "veteran circlers" who shared their stories of encounters with "difficult people" and what they learned from them. Our thanks to Michael Black,

Margie Clark, Diana Hart, Alexandra Hart, Barton Stone, and Joe Ulmer in Sonoma County, California.

Charlie and Cindy wish to acknowledge their colleagues Carol Kleinmaier and Larry Yang at Kairos, Support for Caregivers, in San Francisco for helping to introduce wisdom circles to people with HIV/AIDS and their caregivers. Thank you for "testing" the format successfully in the crucible of an epidemic. You have shown us what compassionate community is really about.

We thank our colleague and friend Lana Angel, who has given her full support to Wisdom Circles since its infancy and who has tested the format in her own circles and given us much excellent feedback. Her wit and honesty are invaluable gifts. We are also indebted to Nancy Thompson, who spent many long hours with Cindy talking about the application of circles to healing the wounds of racism.

We gratefully acknowledge the contribution of Sylvia and Edward Garfield, Rita and Norman Centkowski, and Mary and Bill Garrett—our ancestors from whom we first learned compassion—and that of our two special friends, Jesse Brown III and Josef Casteele, whose bright futures we hope will be enhanced by this book.

Charlie and Cindy offer a special tribute to their cat Parsifal whose loving and playful presence brightened the months of toil on this book. "P," like his Arthurian namesake, was an "innocent fool" and his limitless curiosity led him to an encounter with a coyote. He taught us much about continuing the quest to embrace life fully for as long as we are able.

Many thanks also to Harriet Wright in San Diego, Jennifer Jaffe in Claremont, California, Ginger Campbell in Pelham, Alabama, and Morgan Vail in Sacramento for your sustained commitment to taking wisdom circles into the world. And a hearty thanks to our manuscript reviewers who slogged through an early draft of this book and gave us a bushel of useful comments: Lana Angel, Tom Hurley, Dick Kernen, Bharat Lindemood, Paul Ray, and Harriet Wright.

Our sincere appreciation to Ned Leavitt, our agent, for his determination to find the best publishing house for this book; to Leslie Wells, our editor, for her enthusiasm for this book and excellent suggestions; to Jennifer Lang, David Lott, and Christine Weathersbee and to all the folks at Hyperion for rounding out the circle that brought this book to fruition.

Finally, a deeply felt thank you to all those who have sat with us in circles, taken the wisdom circles format into your homes and organizations, and committed yourselves to a world that works for everyone.